735 WEIRD CRAZY & FUN FACTS

TRIVIA BOOK FOR CURIOUS MINDS

Copyright © 2022 by ReaverCrest Design

First paperback edition January 2022

Book design by ReaverCrest Design

ISBN: 9798794828863

All rights reserved. No part of this book may be reproduced or used in any manner without the prior written permission of the copyright owner.

Trademarked names are used in an editorial fashion, with no intention of infringement of the respective owner's trademark. The information contained within this book is for educational and entertainment purposes only. The content within this book has been derived from various sources. The information in this book was correct at the time of publication. No warranties of any kind are declared or implied.

Neither the author nor the publisher shall have any liability to any person or entity with respect to any loss or damage caused or alleged to be caused directly or indirectly by the information contained in this book. This book does not replace the advice of a medical professional. Consult your physician before making any changes to your diet or regular health plan. Readers acknowledge that the author is not engaged in the rendering of legal, financial, medical or professional advice.

Table Of Contents

Miscellaneous Facts	....	7
ANIMALS	....	23
SCIENCE	....	35
SPACE	....	45
HISTORY	....	51
MUSIC	....	63
TECHNOLOGY	....	71

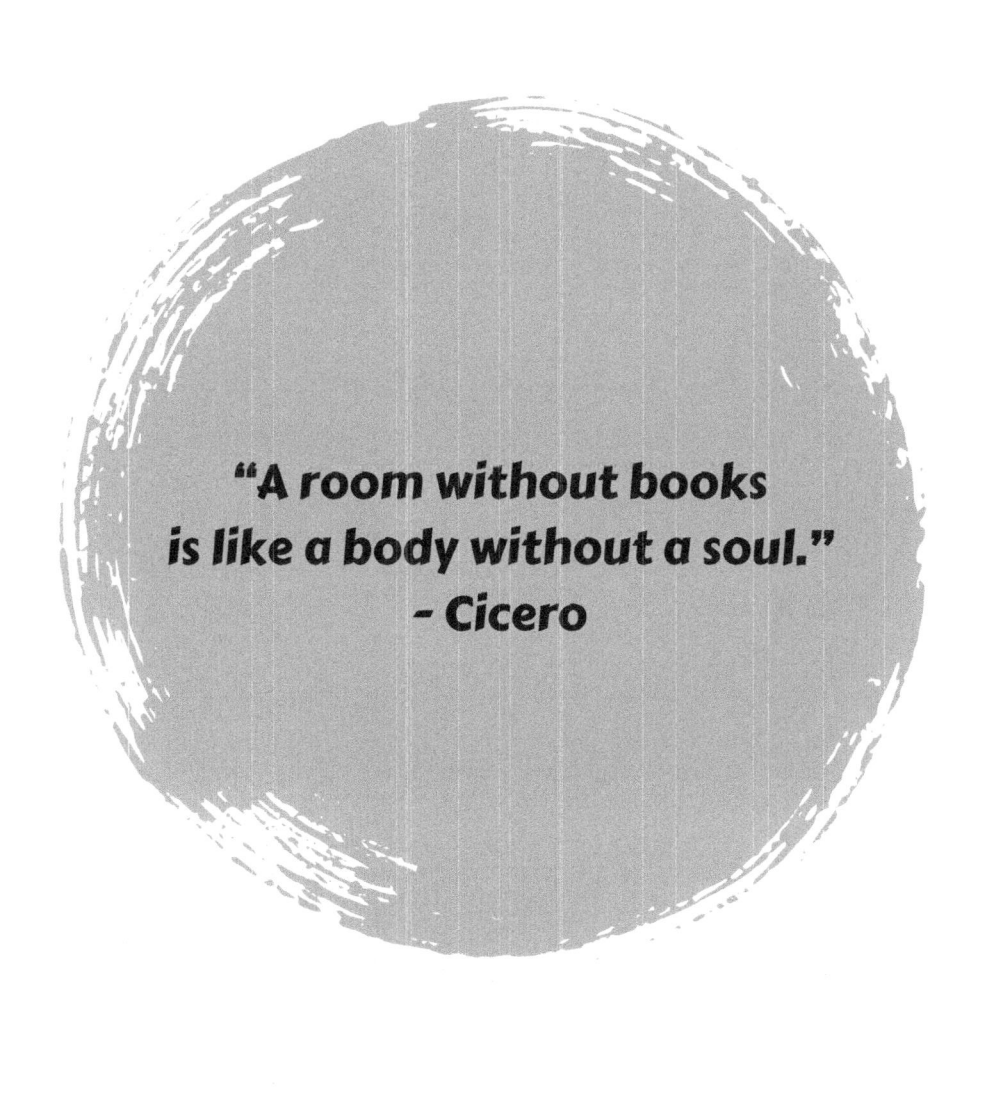

"A room without books
is like a body without a soul."
- Cicero

Miscellaneous Facts

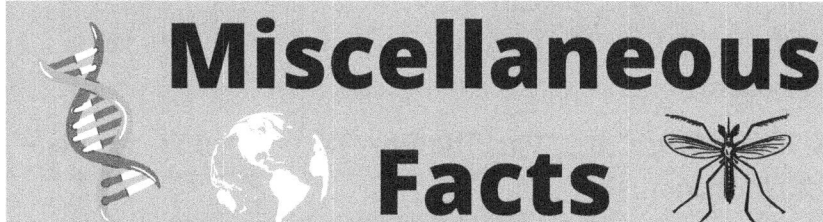

1. The hottest temperature ever recorded occurred in Furnace Creek, Death Valley, California, at 134 degrees Fahrenheit on July 10, 1913.

2. The coldest temperature ever recorded occurred in Antarctica, -144 Fahrenheit, as reported by researchers in a scientific journal in 2018.

3. More people visit France than any other country (Spain is second, the US third).

4. The longest place name in the word, 85 letters, is "Taumatawhakatangihangakoauauotamateaturipukakapikimaungahoronukupokaiwhenuakitanatahu," New Zealand. Locals call it Taumata Hill.

5. The sentence, "The quick brown fox jumps over the lazy dog" uses every letter in the English language.

6. Freelancers originally referred to self-employed, sword-wielding mercenaries, literally "free lancers."

7. People started wearing pajamas, originally spelled "pyjamas," instead of nightgowns so they'd be prepared to run outside in public during World War I air raids in England.

8. The teddy bear is named after President Theodore Roosevelt. After he refused to shoot a captured black bear on a hunt, a stuffed-animal maker (Morris Michtom) decided to create a bear and name it after the president.

9. It takes 570 gallons to paint the exterior of the White House.

10. Buckingham Palace in London, England, has 775 rooms, including 78 bathrooms.

11. The White House in Washington, DC, has 132 rooms, including 35 bathrooms.

12. The first footprints on the moon will remain there for a million years.

13. The tallest building in the world is the Burj Khalifa in Dubai, standing at over 2,722 feet.

14. The biggest pizza ever created was 13,580 square feet, made in Rome, Italy, in 2012. The pizza was gluten-free and named "Ottavia" after a roman emperor.

15. The word "strengths" is the longest word in the English language with only one vowel.

16. According to recent research, the human nose can distinguish at least a trillion different odors.

17. Skin is the body's largest organ.

18. It's impossible to hum while holding your nose.

19. There are no muscles in your fingers. Their function is controlled by muscles in your palms and arms.

20. The wedding of Princess Diana and Prince Charles was watched by 750 million people worldwide in 1981. 2.5 billion watched her funeral in 1997.

21. Psycho is the first U.S. film to feature a toilet flushing.

22. Spreading diseases such as malaria, dengue, West Nile, yellow fever, Zika, chikungunya, and lymphatic filariasis, the mosquito kills more people than any other creature in the world.

23. The mosquito recognized as one of the largest in the world is the Australian elephant mosquito - Toxorhynchites speciosus, which is about 1.5 inches long.

24. During World War II, a Great Dane named Juliana was awarded the Blue Cross Medal. She extinguished an incendiary bomb by peeing on it.

25. There were female Gladiators in Ancient Rome. A female gladiator was called a Gladiatrix, or Gladiatrices. They were extremely rare, unlike their male counterparts.

26. Only 6 people died in the Great Fire of London. Despite destroying over 13,500 houses and displacing 80,000 people, it only claimed the lives of 6 unlucky Londoners.

27. Umbrellas were once only used by women.

28. There are more than 200 languages that have been invented just for television or movies.

29 Over the course of an average lifetime, most people will spend an entire year sitting on the toilet.

30. There's a town in Norway called Hell. Ironically, it never gets very warm there at all.

31. Seven percent of American adults think chocolate milk comes from brown cows.

32. Ketchup was once sold as medicine to treat diarrhea and indigestion.

33. It takes 70 different pieces of wood to make up a violin.

34. The World's Longest Concert by Multiple Artists happened in 2017. It started on March 17th and continued until April 5th. The concert was part of Canada's celebration of their country's 150th anniversary. It lasted for 453 hours, 54 minutes, and 40 seconds.

35. A blind chameleon can still adjust to the colors of its environment. The way it changes colors is because of its special cells, not eyesight.

36. There is only one country on earth without mosquitoes - Iceland.

37. A group of lemurs is called a conspiracy. Lemurs are social animals and live in mini communities of around 10-25 members. As a result of this, they often work together, or 'conspire' to outwit predators using a technique called 'mobbing'.

38. You lose up to 30% of your taste buds during flight. The atmosphere in an airline cabin reduces your ability to detect tastes by about 30 percent.

39. The world's oldest wooden wheel has been around for more than 5,000 years. It was found in 2002, approximately 12 miles south of Ljubljana, the capital of Slovenia, and is now housed in the city's museum.

40. The Pope can't be an organ donor. According to the Vatican, the Pope's entire body must be buried intact because his body belongs to the universal Catholic Church.

41. Adult cats are lactose intolerant.
Like some humans, adult cats don't have enough of the lactase enzyme to digest lactose from milk, causing them to vomit, have diarrhea, or get gassy.

42. Wimbledon tennis balls are kept at 68 degrees Fahrenheit.
The temperature of a tennis ball affects how it bounces. At warmer temperatures, the gas molecules inside the ball expand, making the ball bounce higher. Lower temperatures cause the molecules to shrink and the ball to bounce lower.

43. Martin Luther King Jr. got a C in public speaking. While attending Crozer Theological Seminary in Pennsylvania, he earned a C in public speaking during his first and second term.

44. Pregnancy tests date back to 1350 B.C.E. According to a document written on ancient papyrus, Egyptian women urinated on wheat and barley seeds to determine if they were pregnant or not. If wheat grew, it predicted a female baby. If barley grew, it predicted a male baby.

45. Nikola Tesla hated pearls. Despite his patience with scientific experimentation, he had no tolerance for pearls. When his secretary wore pearl jewelry one day, he made her go home.

46. Irish bars used to be closed on Saint Patrick's Day. Until 1961, there were laws in Ireland that banned bars from opening on March 17. Since the holiday falls during the period of Lent in the heavily Catholic country, the idea of binge-drinking seemed immoral.

47. The first stroller was engineered to be pulled by a goat or animal of similar size. William Kent, a landscape architect, invented the first stroller for the third Duke of Devonshire in 1733.

48. Penicillin was first called "mold juice". In 1928, bacteriologist Alexander Fleming left a petri dish in his lab while he was on vacation, only to return and find that some liquid around the mold had killed the bacteria in the dish. This became the world's first antibiotic.

49. We're one to two centimeters taller in the morning than at night.

50. The human body contains enough fat to make about seven bars of soap.

51. Some blood vessels in a blue whale are big enough for humans to swim through.

52. Babies are born with more bones than adults, babies have 300 bones while adults only have 206.

53. Goosebumps developed to make our ancestors' hair stand up, making them appear more threatening to predators.

54. A sneeze shoots through the air at 100 miles per hour, sending 10,000 germs flying.

55. Stomach acid is strong enough to dissolve metal.

56. In WWII British soldiers had to make do with only three sheets of toilet paper per day.

57. Chickens don't just eat seeds, they like to eat insects and also mice and lizards.

58. Gorillas, monkeys, bonobos, and other primates make a new nest to sleep in every night.

59. Apples come from the same plant family as roses. So do plums, raspberries, and many other fruits.

60. The technical term for a fear of long words is hippopotomonstrosesquippedaliophobia. Sesquipedalophobia is another term for the phobia.

61. Hiking naked is illegal in Switzerland.

62. New York's Central Park is bigger than Monaco.

63. There are over 9,000 benches in Central Park.

64. There are over 700 ancient Egyptian hieroglyphic symbols.

65. A woodpecker's tongue is bigger than its entire head. The green woodpecker's tongue is so long, that it has to coil behind the skull, over the eyes and into the right nostril in order to fit inside the bird's head. It also helps protect the bird's brain from injury during high-speed pecking.

66. The expression "heart of gold" was invented by Shakespeare.

67. To make one pound of honey, a bee has to fly 90,000 miles. One bee typically only makes one-twelfth of a teaspoon of the stuff in its lifetime.

68. Not only are groups of crows called murders, but the birds actually hold funerals for their dead.

69. The heaviest onion on record was grown by Pete Glazebrook of England. It weighed 17 pounds.

70. The oldest domestic cat on record lived for 38 years. She was Creme Puff of Austin, Texas.

71. The longest noodle ever made is more than 10,000 feet long. That's almost two miles.

72. The average human body carries more bacteria cells than human cells.

73. The Supreme Court has its own basketball court, with a nickname - "The highest court in the Land".

74. In their lifetime, the average person walks the equivalent of five times around the Earth.

75. The only letter of the alphabet that doesn't appear in any American state is q.

76. Glaciers, ice caps, and ice sheets hold nearly 69 percent of the world's freshwater.

77. Whale songs can be used by scientists to sonically map out the ocean floor.

78. The first person charged with speeding in a vehicle was going eight miles per hour. In 1896 Walter Arnold of Kent, England, became the first person to be convicted of speeding. He was fined one shilling for speeding at 8 mph (13 km/h), thereby exceeding the contemporary speed limit of 2 mph (3.2 km/h)

79. The last living person who was the child of a Civil War veteran, died in June of 2020. Her father was 83 when she was born.

80. The microgravity in space can cause an astronauts blood to run backwards.

81. Humans create as much heat as a 100 watt incandescent bulb.

82. Multiplying any two digit number with eleven is the sum of the two digit inserted between the two digits - 54×11=> (5+4) => 594 or 36×11=> (3+6) => 396.

83. Since it's discovery in 1930, Pluto has yet to orbit the sun and won't until 2178.

84. In the time it takes you to read this sentence, you've traveled approximately 2,200 miles through space relative to the cosmic background radiation.

85. Your tongue rests on the roof of your mouth, not the base.

86. For 1 600 billionth of a second when a hydrogen bomb detonates, it is 100 million degrees Celsius. The core of the sun is 15 million degrees Celsius.

87. The lighter was invented before the match. The cigarette lighter was invented before the first conventional, friction-based match. The German chemist Johann Dobereiner invented the lighter in 1823 using hydrogen and platinum. The friction-match was invented in 1826 by English chemist John Walker.

88. Crows have extremely good memory, they can even get their relatives to recognize people that they've already recognised.

89. Axolotls can regenerate anything as long as they stay within their original climate and pool of water. If they stay outside of it or the pool changes chemicals, they become salamanders that can't regenerate anymore.

90. The brain is the only thing that we know of that has named itself.

91. A sword made from the blood of your enemies is technically possible. If you separate the iron out of the blood of 300 adults, you could smelt it down to an iron ingot. This ingot would be enough to create a longsword.

92. Diamonds aren't valuable nor are they rare.
Diamonds are not particularly rare. Compared to other gemstones, they're the most common precious stone found. The cost per carat (or weight of a gemstone) is based upon a stone's rarity, the rarer the stone, the more expensive. Rubies, emeralds and sapphires are much rarer and far more expensive than diamonds.

93. Cats don't meow to talk to other cats, they use different language for that. They meow to talk to us.

94. The Sun is extremely loud, we can't hear it because sound can't travel through the vacuum of space.

95. Lemons aren't naturally occuring, they were created through the breeding of bitter oranges and citrons.

96. Juno (unmanned space probe) who was sent to Jupiter by NASA, was Jupiter's wife in Roman mythology. Jupiter's moons are named after Jupiter's mistresses. NASA sent Jupiter's wife to 'spy' on him and his mistresses.

97. Natural redheads have a genetic resistance to anesthesia and unusually high tolerance for pain.

98. Male reindeer lose their antlers in the winter but females don't.

99. There are more people in California than Canada.

100. Australia is wider than the moon. Australia's diameter is 600km wider than the moon's. The moon sits at 3400km in diameter, while Australia's diameter from east to west is almost 4000km.

101. The Hollywood sign in Los Angeles once said "Hollywoodland."

102. According to the latest measurements by the Icelandic National Land Survey, Iceland is expanding at the rate of 2 cm (0.8 inches) each year as the eastern part of Iceland drifts to the east and the western part drifts to the west.

103. The highest concentrations of long caves in the world are found in the Pennyroyal Plateau of southern Kentucky, United States, in the Black Hills of South Dakota and in the Yucatán Peninsula, Mexico.

104. It is physically impossible for pigs to look up into the sky.

105. The "sixth sick sheik's sixth sheep's sick" is the toughest tongue twister in the English language.

106. If you sneeze too hard, you could fracture a rib.

107. Wearing headphones for more than 60 minutes at a go is bad for the ears. When you put on headphones, you cover your ears from the natural air, which increases the production of bacteria by 700% in 1hr.

108. In the course of an average lifetime, while sleeping you might eat around 70 assorted insects and 10 spiders.

109. Most people fall asleep in seven minutes.

110. The giant squid has the largest eyes in the world. In a living colossal squid they measure about 27 cm across, about the size of a soccer ball.

111. In many advertisements, the time displayed on a watch is 10:10.

112. Los Angeles full name is "El Pueblo de Nuestra Senora la Reina de los Angeles de Porciuncula" - "Our Lady the Queen of the Angels of Porciuncula".

113. There are only four words in the English language which end in "dous": tremendous, horrendous, stupendous, and hazardous.

114. "Dreamt" is the only English word that ends with the letters "mt".

115. There are 293 ways to make change for a dollar.

116. Rubber bands last longer when refrigerated.

117. Like fingerprints, everyone's tongue print is different.

118. The largest living organism in the world is a fungus. It is in Oregon, covering 2,200 acres and is still growing.

119. Kangaroos can not walk backwards as they are not capable of moving each leg independently.

120. The shortest war in history lasted for only 38 minutes. Anglo-Zanzibar War of 1896 is considered to be the shortest war in history, lasting for a grand total of 38 minutes.

121. While you sleep you can't smell anything. While sound can disrupt sleep, scents cannot.

122. Your brain uses 10 watts of energy to think and does not feel pain.

123. The nail grows slower in cold weather and faster in warm weather because circulation is slower in the cold weather, causing a growth slow down.

124. The average person spends two weeks of their life waiting at traffic lights.

125. Before 1913 parents could mail their kids to Grandma's, through the postal service.

126. Because of the 4 stages of the Water Cycle – Evaporation, Condensation, Precipitation and Collection – water falling as rain today may have previously fallen as rain days, weeks, months or years before.

127. Birds can not live in space – they need gravity to be able to swallow.

128. Baby koalas are fed poo by their parents after they are born which helps them digest Eucalyptus leaves later in life.

129. Tsunamis can travel at speeds of about 500 miles or 805 kilometers an hour, almost as fast as a jet plane.

130. When you look at a bright sky and see white dots, you are looking at your blood. Those are white blood cells.

131. Cows can walk up stairs but not down them.

132. Tiger shark embryos begin attacking each other in their mother's womb before they are even born.

133. Mars is red because it has a layer of rusty dust covering the whole surface, and, if the scientists are right, it is blowing some of it out into space.

134. 20% of all the oxygen you breathe is used by your brain.

135. Don't eat too many carrots or you will turn orange.

136. Thailand got its name from the Thai people, the ethnic group of the central plains.

137. Vatican City Is the Only Country Designated a World Heritage Site

138. The Olympics was postponed for the first time in modern history. The 2020 Summer Olympics, scheduled to start on July 24 2020, has officially been postponed due to the severe outbreak of COVID-19 worldwide.

139. There are 10 types of green tea - Sencha, Gyokuro, Tencha, Matcha, Funmatsucha, Konacha, Shincha, Fukamushicha, Kukicha and Bancha. Green tea is called as such due to the natural green color of the leaves, and the color of the brew.

140. You can find egg coffee in Vietnam. Vietnam is the second-largest coffee producer in the world. You can find many different types of coffee, hot and iced, in different parts of the country. Most noteworthy is the egg coffee (ca phe trung), a specialty in North Vietnam. Egg coffee is made using dark coffee topped with egg yolk and condensed milk, whipped together to create an airy froth on top.

141. The term T-shirt first appeared in a novel in 1920. F. Scott Fitzgerald was the first known person to use the term T-shirt when he included it in his novel, This Side of Paradise.

142. The hashtag symbol is technically called an octothorpe. According to the Merriam-Webster dictionary, the "octo-" prefix refers to the eight points on the popular symbol, but the "thorpe" remains a mystery. One theory claims that it comes from the Old English word for "village," based on the idea that the symbol looks like a village surrounded by eight fields.

143. The 100 folds in a chef's hat represent 100 ways to cook an egg. The pleats used to signify a chef's level of experience, like the number of ways he or she knew how to prepare eggs.

144. The longest wedding veil was longer than 63 football fields - nearly 23,000 feet, which is the same length as about 63.5 football fields.

145. Apple Pie isn't actually American at all. Neither apple pies nor apples originally came from America. Apples are native to Asia, and the first recorded recipe for apple pie was actually written in England.

146. Google Images was created because of Jennifer Lopez.
When Jennifer Lopez wore a green Versace dress to the 42nd Grammy Awards, it was so iconic that the dress became the top search in the history of Google at the time. Because of such high demand that couldn't be handled by the regular Google search, Google Images was introduced on July 12, 2001.

147. The most visited website in the world is Google. Number of monthly visits in billions - 86.9. google.com is ranked #1 as the most visited website in the world for November 2021.

148. There are more than 3 million shipwrecks on the ocean floors. And less than 1% of them have been explored. It is estimated that more than $60 billion of treasures are in these shipwrecks.

149. Marshmallows used to be a delicacy for gods and royalty.
As early as 2000 BC during ancient Egyptian times, the Egyptians extracted sap from the mallow plants and mixed the sap with nuts and honey to make marshmallows.

150. Everyone with blue eyes are related. Scientists in Copenhagen University have found that 6,000 to 10,000 years ago, everyone had brown eyes. Due to a sudden mutation of the OCA2 gene, blue eyes were formed! From this, they were able to conclude that all blue-eyed people are related to the same ancestor.

151. The Titanic took 2 hours 40 minutes to sink. And that's the same duration as the length of the movie 'Titanic', without the present-day scenes and end credits.

152. The headquarters of the United Nations is in New York City. Founded after World War 2, the United Nations, or commonly known as the UN, was formed to replace the League of Nations. Overseeing the East River, the UN headquarters is a complex located in the Turtle Bay neighborhood of Manhattan.

153. The national flag of Nepal is the only non-rectangular flag in the world. The Nepalese flag is made up of two pennons, instead of the common quadrilateral flag similar to other countries in the world. The national flag is both its state flag and civil flag of the sovereign nation.

154. The youngest mother in history was only 5 years old. Lina Medina from Peru was born in 1933, and she was less than 5 years old when she became pregnant. She was 5 years, 7 months and 21 days old when she gave birth to her son.

155. Beer cans in Japan are stamped with Braille. This is an initiative from beer companies in Japan to prevent the blind from consuming alcohol by mistake.

156. The word "Tip" originally meant "To Insure Promptitude". The practice of tipping may have started since the late Middle Ages, but the word "tip" probably originated from Samuel Johnson. In the cafe that Johnson often frequented, a bowl labeled "To Insure Promptitude" was available for guests to drop coins for better service. This phrase was shortened to "T.I.P.", which eventually became the word "tip" in modern days.

157. The Grand Canyon is more than 1-mile deep. Attracting more than 6 million visitors annually, the Grand Canyon is located by the Colorado River in Arizona, United States. The Grand Canyon is 277 miles (or 446 km) long, 18 miles (29 km) wide and 6093 feet (1857 m) deep.

158. In 2014, at 17 years, Malala Yousafzai became the youngest person to receive a Nobel Prize. Malala Yousafzai from Pakistan won the Nobel Peace Prize in 2014 for her struggle against the suppression of children and young people, and the right for all children to receive education.

159. The name of the CPR dummy is Annie. Also known as the "most kissed" face of all time, the CPR mannequin face was inspired by the mask, L'Inconnue de la Seine (The Unknown Woman of the Seine). When Peter Safar, an Austrian physician, and Asmund Laerdal, a Norwegian toymaker were making the mannequin in 1958, Laerdal was bewitched by the face hanging on the wall of his parents' house.

160. RSVP stands for "Répondez, s'il vous plaît". This French phrase simply means "Please respond".

161. The Trans-Siberian railroad crosses 16 large rivers, including the Volga, the Irtysh, the Kama, the Ob, the Yenisei, the Amur, and some others. The total number of bridges that the train passes from start to finish is 3901.

162. Juliet is 13 years old in the play Romeo and Juliet. Whereas Romeo's age remains a mystery in the play.

163. The longest living insect is the termite queen. The termite queen can live up to 50 years, making it the insect with the longest lifespan. Its egg production is at its peak for almost 10 years.

164. Antarctica is classified as a desert due to its low rainfall. Antarctica is also the largest desert on Earth, with a total land size of 14 million square kilometers. The average annual rainfall in Antarctica was only 10 mm over the last 30 years.

165. Earth has experienced 5 mass extinctions. The first mass extinction happened as early as 444 million years ago, called the Ordovician-Silurian extinction. The subsequent mass extinctions are Late Devonian extinction, Permian-Triassic extinction, Triassic-Jurassic extinction, and Cretaceous-Paleogene extinction.

166. There are more than 1000 editions of the Monopoly board game. First published in 1935 by Hasbro, this popular property trading board game has been sold in more than 114 countries worldwide.

167. The creator of I ♥ NY designed the logo in the back of a taxi. Milton Glaser was hired to design a logo for New York city to boost tourism.

168. 4.54 billion people use the internet. That's over half of the world's population.

169. 10% of all the photos ever taken came from the past few years.
Yes, we're talking about all of the photos ever taken since the beginning of photography. Considering how photography started in the 1800s, 10% is a pretty big chunk.

170. Australia has more than 10,000 beaches. With over 50,000 kilometers of coastline, Australia holds the record for the most number of beaches. The entire coastline is joined by over 10,000 beaches and it will take you at least 27 years to visit all of these beaches.

171. Snake Island in Brazil is a snake island, literally. Habitat to more than 5000 golden lanceheads, Ilha da Queimada Grande is home to these snakes. The golden lancehead pit viper is one of the world's most dangerous and venomous snake species. The venom is so deadly that even a single drop eats away human flesh.

172. The Universe expands 14.8 km per minute. Even with all the knowledge we have on space, only 4% of the observable universe has been studied so far.

173. Shakespeare created the name "Jessica." His legacy not only lives in his timeless literature, but for the words and names he crafted. One such name is Jessica, which Shakespeare created for The Merchant Of Venice.

174. The inventor of roller skates crashed a party wearing them as a first demo. John Joseph Merlin is known as the inventor of roller skates in 1760. He debuted his invention at a fancy party where he skated in while playing the violin. Eventually, he crashed into a £500 mirror.

175. The world's deepest postbox lies over 30 feet underwater.
The world's deepest mailbox can be found off the coast of Susami Bay, Japan. This underwater postbox is used by divers to send postcards to their friends and family. To make sure that the waterproof postcards are delivered, a clerk checks the mailbox regularly.

176. Armadillos always give birth to quadruplets.

ANIMALS

177. With a single bite, king cobras may inject up to 7 milliliters (about 1.5 teaspoons) of venom into their victims. A small amount, such as two-tenths of a fluid ounce, can kill 20 humans or even an elephant. The venom affects the brain's respiratory centers directly, causing heart failure.

178. There are over ten quadrillion ants on Earth. According to scientists, there are around 1.5 million ants for every human on the planet.

179. The golden poison dart frog (Phyllobates terribilis) is about the size of a paperclip. Its skin is coated with a fatal poison that renders its victims' nerves and muscles inert, resulting in death. This tiny frog has around one milligram of poison, which is enough to kill 10 to 20 people if it enters their bloodstreams.

180. Cape buffaloes (Syncerus caffer) are extremely dangerous because of their unpredictable nature. That, plus their sheer strength and robust physique can knock out prey in an instant. They stalk and circle their prey before charging at speeds of up to 56 kilometers per hour

181. At least eight species of horned lizard (Phrynosoma) can aim and squirt blood from their eyes. They restrict the blood flow to their head until the pressure builds up, rupturing the vessels in their eyelids. They do this as a defence mechanism to confuse their predators.

182. Hummingbirds are the only birds that can fly backwards.

183. Squirrels plant thousands of new trees each year by merely forgetting where they put their acorns.

184. Turtles Breathe Out of Their Butt.
Technically the term is cloacal respiration, and it's not so much breathing as just diffusing oxygen in and carbon dioxide out, but the fact remains: when turtles hibernate, their main source of oxygen is through their butt.

185. Sea otters hold hands when they sleep to keep from drifting apart. To prevent themselves from floating away in the swirling sea while they sleep, sea otters often entangle themselves in forests of kelp or giant seaweed to provide anchorage. This is also the reason why they hold hands. They do so in order to prevent themselves from drifting away from the group.

186. When playing with female puppies, male puppies will often let them win, even if they have a physical advantage.

187. Cows have best friends.
Research from the University of Northampton has highlighted the human-like relationships among cattle. The research found that cattle have selective friendships, and experience significantly less stress when they are hanging out with their mates.

188. Penguins propose to their lifemates with a pebble.
During courtship, the male will present the female with a pebble as a gift. Penguins live on rocky shores and prize these small stones to build their nests during mating season. If the female accepts the generous gift, they bond and mate for life.

189. Macaques in Japan use coins to buy vending machine snacks.

190. Ghost crabs growl using teeth in their stomachs.

191. The world's oldest known breed of domesticated dog dates back to 329 BC.

192. The oldest evidence of domesticated cats dates back 9,500 years.

193. Norway knighted a penguin.
Brigadier Sir Nils Olav III is a king penguin who resides in Edinburgh Zoo, Scotland. He is the mascot and colonel-in-chief of the Norwegian King's Guard. The first Nils Olav died in 1987, but he was replaced with another penguin, called Nils Olav II. He kept getting promoted, and in 2008 he was even knighted, which was approved by the king of Norway, Harald V.

194. In China, killing a panda is punishable by death.
Prior to 2011, even smuggling a panda could yield such a harsh penalty. In 1987, the Chinese government warned citizens that killing a giant panda could results in long jail terms or even the death penalty.

195. Sweden has a rabbit show-jumping competition called Kaninhoppning. It is typically conducted in a closed, indoor arena, with obstacles scaled to suit the rabbits.

196. The longest orgasm in mammals is that of the domestic pig - Sus scrofa domesticus. On average, it's orgasm lasts 30 minutes, but it can last for as long as 90 minutes.

197. Dolphins have names for each other.
Scientists have found further evidence that dolphins call each other by "name". Research has revealed that the marine mammals use a unique whistle to identify each other.

198. Oysters can change gender depending on which is best for mating. All oysters start off as male, but most change permanently to female by the time they are a year old. Their reproductive organs produce both sperm and eggs, and they can change gender at will. It is technically possible, therefore, for an oyster to fertilize its own eggs.

199. Japanese Macaques make snowballs for fun.

200. Some cats are allergic to people.

201. You can hear a blue whale's heartbeat from more than 2 miles away. The world's largest animal's heart weighs about 400 pounds — approximately the size of a small piano.

202. The unicorn is the national animal of Scotland. Although it's a fabled creature, the national animal of Scotland is the mythical unicorn — chosen because of its association with dominance and chivalry as well as purity and innocence in Celtic mythology.

203. One species of jellyfish, called the Turritopsis Dohrnii, is immortal. It has the ability to revert to its child state after becoming sexually mature, therefore it never dies.

204. Snails can sleep in hibernation for up to three years. They need moist weather to survive. If their environment does not agree with them, they sleep up to three years to escape warm climates.

205. African elephants have a special alarm call when they sense a danger by humans. A study in Kenya showed that elephants had a distinctive low rumble when running away from humans.

206. The now extinct giant penguin, which lived more than 35 million years ago, was the largest ever, roughly 250 pounds in weight and 6 feet 6 inches tall.

207. The arctic reindeer is the only mammal on earth that changes eye colours in different seasons. During summers, its eyes are a dazzling golden, while in winter, its eyes become dark blue to help its vision in low light.

208. The dominant female meerkat (Suricata suricatta) in a clan controls breeding and kills the young of those that aren't her own, ensuring that her own offspring has the best chance of survival.

209. Cone snails (Conus) have one of the world's most painful and fatal 'stings'. They fire a harpoon that can cause muscle paralysis and respiratory failure. Nicknamed the 'cigarette snail', its victims are said to only have enough time to smoke a cigarette before death.

210. You're more likely to be killed by a cow than a shark. More people die annually from getting kicked or stepped on by a cow. Also, it's said that cows all over the world, simultaneously face the same direction while grazing.

211. Sea otters are cute. They can also be aggressive killers. There have been reports that these lovable sea otters (Enhydra lutris) are serial harassers. When males mate, they'll grab the female and aggressively bite her face.

212. Aptly named vampire bats, the most common one feeds solely on the blood of mammals, including humans. They'll identify a warm spot on your skin to bite then create an incision with their razor-sharp teeth, lapping up the blood from the wound.

213. Humans and chimps share 96% of DNA. The DNA sequence that can be directly compared between the two genomes is almost 99 percent identical. When DNA insertions and deletions are taken into account, humans and chimps still share 96 percent of their sequence.

214. Animal waste is 30 times greater than human waste, generating around 1.4 billion tons yearly.

215. Female ferrets can die if they do not mate once they go into heat. If mating does not occur, the females will succumb to aplastic anemia and die a most painful death.

216. Dolphins use toxic pufferfish to 'get high'. Pufferfish produce a potent defensive chemical, which they eject when threatened.

217. Ants have two stomachs.
They use one to feed themselves, while the other stomach can be used to nurture others. This process of feeding among ants through their second stomach is called trophallaxis.

218. Anteaters are toothless carnivores.
As edentate animals, anteaters do not need teeth in catching their prey. Instead, they use their narrow tongues which can go up to 2 feet long. The small spines and sticky saliva on their tongues enable them to catch ants and termites easily.

219. Part of the arctic fox diet is its own waste.
As they digest the food a second time, the arctic fox can then extract extra nourishment. They also eat the waste of other animals. Moreover, eating waste helps the arctic fox in keeping their salt levels in balance.

220. The hatching of barn owl eggs is asynchronous.
It means that each egg hatches exactly 30 days from when it was laid. Hence, some chicks end up being either younger or older by a few weeks than their siblings. The number of laid barn owl eggs may vary from 4-7 in normal cases, but with recorded cases of up to 14 eggs laid.

221. Among the mammals on earth, the bat is the slowest in terms of reproduction.
They only start reproducing by age 2 with a typical production count of only one offspring each year. Bat gestation periods can last from 40 days to 6 months. Autumn and winter are the mating seasons for bats, with the females carrying the males' sperm during winter until they ovulate in spring and become pregnant.

222. Reindeer milk contains more fat content than cow milk.

223. Adult lions pretend to be hurt by the bites of their young to encourage their strength.

224. Rats are not physically capable of vomiting, hence why Rat Poison is so effective.

225. The bearded dragon has an essential beard for a reason.
Both male and female bearded dragons have beards, and they use them in communication processes. When threatened, for one, they open their mouths, raise their chins, and puff the beard out to generate a bigger appearance. A hiss usually accompanies this display.

226. The beaver has a specially designed body for its semi-aquatic lifestyle.
They spend their time divided between land and water. Due to its stiff tail and webbed feet, the beaver can efficiently move through the water. Moreover, its thick, waterproof coating keeps out the cold even when it is swimming.

227. The Bengal tiger have built-in first aid kit.
The natural antiseptic contents of its saliva prevent infections on wounds. Thus, healing from injury is fast for a Bengal tiger.

228. Among all predators on Earth, the brown bear is the only species that eat both meat and plants.
It is the reason why the brown bear has 2 separate sets of teeth that they use for each of the types of food they eat.

229. Camel humps are adaptable fat storages.
These distinctive body parts of the camel grow into mini hills when filled with food and water and diminish in size upon the usage of the stored fat.

230. Cats are superior to dogs when it comes to intelligence.
The cerebral cortex of cats contains around 300 million neurons while dogs only have 160 million. Cats can also make different sounds with 10 times more types than dogs do. While cats are more able to solve difficult cognitive problems, dogs still have higher social IQs.

231. Snakes always keep their eyes open, even when they are asleep. Snakes shed their eye scale as part of the shedding process. They sleep with their eyes open because they do not have any eyelids.

232. Cheetah vision sees from 3 miles away.
While its sense of smell is at par with its sense of sight, the cheetah utilizes its superior vision as its main weapon when hunting. Even the sun is not much of an obstacle as the tear mark beneath its eyes are specially designed to keep the sunlight away.

233. Chicken vision is better than that of humans.
Human eyes possess only 3 cone types, enabling the sight for blue, green, and red color. Meanwhile, chickens have additional 2 cone types, allowing them to detect violet and ultraviolet light. Their ability to see the sunrise about an hour before humans can is the reason why chickens crow early in the morning.

234. The color of eggs that chickens produce is predictable from their ear lobe colors. Brown eggs hail from chickens with red ear lobes while white eggs lay from chickens with white ear lobes.

235. A headless cockroach can still survive for up to two weeks.
Unlike other insects, the cockroach has its brain inside its body instead of its head. This unique body feature enables the cockroach to still have control over the rest of its body even with the absence of its head.

236. Despite being a wild cat, the cougar does not have the ability to roar. The cougar would purr like a domesticated house cat instead, regardless of its being a fierce cat by nature.

237. Dog nose prints are as unique as human thumbprints.
It might as well serve as the individual identification for every single dog on the planet. Upon closer look, one can see the distinctive serial bumps and ridges on their noses.

238. Ostriches can run faster than horses, and the males can roar like lions.

239. Crickets have ears on their front legs.

240. Elephants can run up to 25 miles per hour. However, they remain the only mammal on earth that can't jump. They always keep one leg on the ground - even when running.

241. Dolphins are susceptible to drowning.
As mammals, dolphins can only breathe by coming to the surface, depriving them of the luxuries of deep sleep in the ocean. Hence, they have to choose between 2 sleeping methods. Dolphins can sleep either by resting vertically or horizontally in the water or by sleeping while swimming slowly alongside another dolphin.

242. The superior visual range of dragonflies comes with the ability to see across several spectrums.
The three opsins in human eyes allow for seeing the visible rainbow colors. Meanwhile, dragonflies have five opsins, making them able to see UV light that is invisible to human eyes.

243. A sleeping duck can keep one of its eyes open and control which brain side stays awake.
Duck flocks normally sleep side by side, forming a long row. Usually, the ducks at each end leave the eye facing away from the row open. It lets them rest while still literally keeping an eye open for possible dangers.

244. Elephants boast of having very developed memories.
Like humans, elephants have the ability to hold grudges, remember past grievances, remember loved ones who have died, and even hold rituals to honor their dead. Elephants also remember old friends who have strayed and returned.

245. The flamingo eats upside-down. They feed by combing their feet through the mud and catching it in their beaks while hanging their heads upside-down. The curved bill of the flamingo features a special design that filters food from water and mud.

246. A dung beetle is the world's strongest insect and also the strongest animal on the planet compared to body weight.

247. Rhinoceros Beetles can lift something 850 times their own weight.

248. The digestive tract of a goldfish does not have a stomach. They only need to consume small quantities of food, hence, it is crucial not to overfeed them. Goldfish must eat at least 5 times per day.

249. Grasshoppers have five eyes. Either side of the head of the grasshopper has a large eye packed with thousands of lenses, enabling them to see in all directions. Moreover, the grasshopper has one eye at the base of each antenna, and then another between the two antennae.

250. The hippopotamus sweats blood. While it is not real blood, the clear liquid that the skin of the hippopotamus secretes turns red to orange until it turns brown. The 'blood' fluid serves as bacteria protection, sunlight reflector, sunscreen, moisturizer, and disinfectant.

251. The tail of a lemur is longer than the length of its body. When the lemur walks, it holds and arches its tail above its head. This gesture gives the lemur more balance as they walk or run and is also essential in moving around in high trees and in communicating with other lemurs.

252. A typical day for a lion consists of 16 to 20 hours of sleep. As nocturnal animals, the lion hunts after dusk with nothing much to do during the day. The lion prepares for the evening as soon as the sun sets as it is also their time to groom and socialize.

253. The lobster executes waste excretion from their faces. Located at the base of its second antennae, openings on the face of the lobster serve as the exit door for its urine. The green glands are the organs from where the lobster excretes waste, and it includes a sac linked to its bladder.

254. The scales of the pangolin are made of the same material as that of human fingernails.

255. Rats laugh when they're tickled.

256. Tuna has the highest protein content for fish. Bluefin and yellowfin tuna are especially rich in protein. Bluefin offers 29.91 grams of protein per 100 grams, and yellowfin provides 29.15 grams.

257. Female animals can sometimes reject sperm. For different species such as chickens, some animals practice sperm dumping to reject the sperm of mates they don't like.

258. There are an estimated 8.7 million species on earth and more than 80% of them are undiscovered.

259. Giant vampire bats lived 100,000 years ago and had a wingspan of 50cm (20 inches).

260. The wood frog spends 7 months of the year frozen.
These Alaskan frogs freeze almost completely at the start of winter, with two-thirds of their body water turning into ice. Their heart stops beating, and their blood flow stops. Once winter starts to thaw so do they and they hop back to life.

261. Emperor penguins are the world's biggest penguins - they are approximately 120cm tall (about the height of a six year old child) and weigh in at around 40 kg. They trek 50–120 km across the Antarctic to reach breeding colonies.

262. Meerkat parents train their offspring to hunt scorpions.
They will bring back dead or almost dead scorpions back to the younger ones so that they can practice killing them without getting stung.

263. Elephants mourn their dead. Elephants will return to the place where family members died and stand in silence over the bones, sometimes bowing their heads.

264. The patu digua is thought to be the smallest spider in the world at just 0.37 mm. This Colombian spider is about one fifth the size of the head of a pin.

265. Wojtek the bear was a corporal in the polish military during WWII. Wojtek became a mascot for his unit. Soldiers would box and wrestle with the bear, who was also fond of smoking and drinking.

266. Pea Crabs are miniature crabs that spend their whole lives inside oysters, clams, and mussels. This tiny crab relies entirely on its host for food.

267. The Mariana snailfish is the deepest fish in the ocean, living up to around 8000m below the surface.

268. Greenland sharks are the longest living vertebrates on earth, with one individual thought to be over 400 years old

269. Dracula ants can snap their mandibles at speeds up to 200 miles per hour - 295 feet per second. That makes it the fastest animal movement on record.

270. The Alpine Swift is able to stay airborne for over 6 months without touching down. It holds the world record for the longest recorded uninterrupted flight by a bird, at over 200 days in the air.

271. A tigers rear legs are so powerful, that they have been found remaining to stand even after death.

272. The smell of a skunk is powerful enough for a human to smell it up to 3.5 miles (5.6 km) away.

273. Great white sharks can detect a drop of blood in 25 gallons (100 litres) of water and can even sense tiny amounts of blood from 3 miles (5 km) away.

274. Giant anteaters consume up to 35,000 ants and termites in a single day.

275. Giraffes are the tallest land animal in the world, reaching heights of 19ft (5.8 m). The ostrich is the world's tallest bird. It can grow up to 9 feet (2.7m) tall.

276. The Giant Pacific Octopus has 3 hearts, 9 brains and blue blood. They are also able to change their colour and texture to camouflage themselves in a blink of an eye.

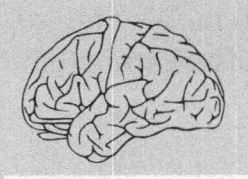

SCIENCE

277. If every star in the Milky Way was a grain of salt they would fill an Olympic sized swimming pool.

278. Micro-organisms have been brought back to life after being frozen in permafrost for three million years.

279. Our oldest radio broadcasts of the 1930s have already travelled past 100,000 stars.

280. To escape the Earth's gravity a rocket need to travel at 7 miles per second or about 25,000 miles per hour.

281. A typical hurricane produces the energy equivalent to 8,000 one megaton bombs.

282. 90% of those who die from hurricanes die from drowning.

283. In the 14th century the Black Death killed 75,000,000 people. It was carried by fleas on the black rat.

284. The mortality rate if bitten by a Black Mamba snake is over 95%.

285. The deepest part of any ocean in the world is the Mariana trench in the Pacific with a depth of 35,797 feet.

286. Marie Curie is the only person to win the Nobel Prize in two different sciences. She was awarded her first Nobel Prize in Physics in 1903 for her work on radiation, and a Nobel Prize in Chemistry in 1911 for her discovery and work on radium and polonium.

287. When you donate your body to science, it can be used as a crash test dummy, a cadaver for medical training, a specimen for forensic research, or a donor for organ transplants.

288. Human cells make up only 43% of the body's total cell count. The rest are bacteria, viruses, and fungi.

289. The human eye has a 576-megapixel resolution. We only see at about 150 dpi, since that is more than enough visual stimuli for us to see objects.

290. Laika was the first animal in space. Two months after Sputnik 1, the Soviet Union launched its second spacecraft, Sputnik 2 with its first passenger - a small dog named Laika.

291. 2 is the only even prime number. A prime number is a special number that is only divisible by 1 and itself. 2 is a prime number that is divisible by 1 and 2.

292. Hot water freezes more quickly than cold water.
The principle of hot liquids freezing faster than cold ones is called the Mpemba effect.

293. Not all diamonds are colorless. Rare diamonds come in different shades of red, green, orange, yellow, brown, black, pink and blue.

294. Spider silk is among the strongest and toughest materials in the natural world, as strong as some steel alloys with a toughness even greater than bulletproof Kevlar.

295. Thales of Miletus was the first physicist. He believed the world was only built from one element: water.

296. The entire human race can fit inside a sugar cube.
If we removed all the spaces between the particles in our atoms, the whole of humanity could be compressed into a singular sugar cube. Almost all of ordinary matter (99.9999999% of it) is empty space.

297. Sound is visible. Any time you see a vibration, you are seeing sound. This is not because sound is invisible, but is because air is invisible. When you talk, you are sending sound waves into the air and the air itself is what is doing the vibrating.

298. Inertia keeps you from falling out of a rollercoaster.
Your mass resists the acceleration of intense loops and keeps you on your seat.

299. You can't sink in the Dead Sea. The Dead Sea has a very high density because of its salt content, which would make it impossible for you to sink.

300. The human stomach can dissolve razor blades.

301. A laser can get trapped in water when you point a laser beam at a jet of flowing water. When the light travels through the water, it is slowed by the heavier particles in the water, effectively "trapping" the laser beam in the water. Even as the water flow is decreased, the laser beam remains contained inside the jet.

302. Scientists estimate that 50-80% of the oxygen production on Earth comes from the ocean. The majority of this production is from oceanic plankton — drifting plants, algae, and some bacteria that can photosynthesize.

303. Animals use Earth's magnetic field for orientation. There is evidence that some animals, like sea turtles and salmon, have the ability to sense the Earth's magnetic field and can use this sense for navigation.

304. The average cumulus cloud can weigh up to a million pounds. That's about as heavy as the world's largest jet when it's completely full of cargo and passengers.

305. Soil is full of life. In just one teaspoon of soil, there are more microorganisms than people on the planet.

306. Bananas are radioactive. Bananas contain potassium, and since potassium decays, that makes the yellow fruit slightly radioactive. You'd need to eat ten million bananas in one sitting to die of banana-induced radiation poisoning.

307. There are more trees on Earth than stars in our galaxy. There could be anywhere from 100 billion to 400 billion stars in the Milky Way. Number of trees around the world is much higher - 3.04 trillion.

308. Men are more likely to be colorblind than women.

309. Humans have genes from other species. Our genome consists of as many as 145 genes that have jumped from bacteria, fungi, other single-celled organisms, and viruses, according to a study published in the journal Genome Biology.

310. It can rain diamonds on other planets.
The atmospheres in Neptune, Uranus, and Saturn have such extreme pressure that they can crystallize carbon atoms and turn them into diamonds.

311. There were roughly 2.5 billion T. rexes on Earth, but not all at the same time. According to the team at the University of California, Berkeley, approximately 2.5 billion of these dinosaurs existed across more than 127,000 generations.

312. Water can exist in three states at once. This is called the triple boil or triple point and it is a specific temperature and pressure where materials exist as a gas, a liquid, and a solid simultaneously.

313. Solar flares are incredibly powerful. The energy solar flares release is equivalent to millions of 100-megaton atomic bombs exploding at once.

314. It's impossible to burp in space. When you burp on Earth, gravity keeps down the solids and liquids from the food you ate, only the gas escapes from your mouth. In the absence of gravity, the gas cannot separate from the liquids and solids, so burping turns into puking.

315. We have no idea what most of the universe looks like. About 96 percent of the universe is made up of dark matter and dark energy, which are undetectable to humans.

316. Beer is twice as fizzy as champagne. While one flute of champagne produces about one million bubbles, a half-pint of beer creates around two million bubbles

317. Sound creates heat. Sound waves generate heat when they travel and are absorbed by materials.

318. Time goes faster at the top of the building than at the bottom. According to Einstein's theory of Relativity, the farther an object is from the Earth's surface, the faster time passes.

319. The sun doesn't change color during sunset. We see it that way because the sun's wavelengths react to the different substances in the atmosphere.

320. Stephen Hawking never won a Nobel Prize.
Despite his extensive work as a theoretical physicist and cosmologist, Stephen Hawking never received any Nobel Prizes.

321. Athanasius Kircher was a scientist who believed in mythological beasts. He strongly believed in mermaids, giants, and dragons.

322. The density of ice is 10% lower than that of water. This explains why ice floats on water.

323. Isaac Newton predicted the world will end in 2060.
Based on a Bible passage, Newton believed that the apocalypse will come some time after the year 2060.

324. Kilauea volcano on Hawaii is the world's most active volcano, followed by Etna in Italy and Piton de la Fournaise on La Réunion island.

325. The Pacific Ocean is the largest and deepest of the world ocean basins. Covering approximately 63 million square miles and containing more than half of the free water on Earth, the Pacific is by far the largest of the world's ocean basins.

326. Galileo Galilei pioneered science through developing the earliest experimental scientific method and the functional telescope.

327. The only letter that doesn't appear on the periodic table is J.

328. Researchers have discovered a new system which transforms urine into electricity using a microbial fuel cell. Just over half a litre of urine is enough for six hours of charge time, which can power a smartphone for three hours.

329. If you get exposed to nuclear substances, the best course of action is to remove all of your clothes. This will remove 90% of the radioactive substance you were exposed to.

330. Tradinno is a giant, animatronic, fire-breathing dragon, the world largest walking robot. It plays the Dragon in the play Drachenstich in the German town of Furth im Wald. The name Tradinno is a mix of Tradition and innovation.

331. The most decimal places of Pi memorised is 70,000, and was achieved by Rajveer Meena (India) at the VIT University, Vellore, India, on 21 March 2015. Rajveer wore a blindfold throughout the entire recall, which took nearly 10 hours.

332. Brain freeze is scientifically known as "Sphenopalatine ganglioneuralgia."

333. It may be colorless in its gas form, but solid and liquid oxygen has a pale blue color.

334. Gasoline can contain between 150 and 1,000 different chemical compounds.

335. 87% of scientists believe that climate change is mostly caused by human activity. Only 50% of the public believes humans caused climate change.

336. The average person has 5 liters of blood. Once a person loses 40% of their blood, they will die without immediate transfusion.

337. Tomatoes have more genes than humans. The tomato contains 31,760 genes – that is 7,000 more genes than a human.

338. The earth has been around for around four to five billion years, humans have only been around for between 0.1 – 0.2% of the time that Earth has existed.

339. An eighth continent, called Zealandia, is hidden under New Zealand and the surrounding Pacific. Since 94% of Zealandia is submerged, discerning the continent's age and mapping it is difficult.

340. The largest tsunami ever recorded occurred in Lituya Bay, Alaska in 1958. The huge wave measured 1720 feet.

341. Alfred Nobel was born into extreme poverty. His work with science led him to produce dynamite and other explosives. He establish the Nobel Peace Prize in 1895.

342. More carbon dioxide has been recorded in the atmosphere today than at any point in the last 800,000 years.

343. Global warming is affecting gravity. The rapid rate of ice melting in Antarctica is so large in scale that it caused a small shift in gravity in the region.

344. A 5th-grader accidentally created a new molecule in 2012. During a class activity, 10-year-old Clara Lazen presented her teacher with a randomly constructed molecule diagram. Instead of dismissing it, Mr. Kenneth Boer took a photo and sent it to a chemist for analysis. Turns out, it was a new, explosive molecule called Tetranitratoxycarbon.

345. According to the National Ocean Service, our oceans hold 20 million pounds of gold, suspended in normal seawater. Currently, there is no efficient way to retrieve these gold deposits from the ocean.

346. It is scientifically possible to die from drinking too much water. When a dehydrated person drinks too much water without the accompanying electrolytes, they can die from water intoxication and hyponatremia.

347. Swimmers sweat underwater. During intense workouts, the body will perspire even in the water.

348. Fast food restaurant ice is often dirtier than toilet water. In a 2016 study conducted in the U.K., major fast-food chains were revealed to have fecal bacteria in their ice.

349. Humans haven't stop evolving. Because humans take so long to reproduce, it takes hundreds to thousands of years for changes in humans to become evident.

350. Tooth enamel is stronger than bones. The lining of our teeth is the hardest substance in the human body.

351. It takes 6 minutes for brain cells to react to alcohol.

352. Humans are the only species known to blush, a behavior Darwin called "the most peculiar and the most human of all expressions."

353. Astronauts can grow up to two inches taller while they're in space.

354. You are always looking at your nose; your brain just chooses to ignore it. While your nose is always in your field of vision, your brain filters it out because it's not information you need to function on a day-to-day basis.

355. You can't tickle yourself.

356. Everyone has their own unique smell, except identical twins.

357. Humans need saliva to be able to taste food.

358. A human produces enough saliva throughout their life to fill two swimming pools.

359. An individual blood cell takes about 60 seconds to make a complete circuit of the body.

360. Charles Osborne spent 68 years of his life hiccuping. He broke a blood vessel in his brain when he fell. He damaged the part of his brain that may have inhibited the hiccup response.

361. The urine of a diabetic person contains so much sugar that it can be purified and made into whiskey.

362. The nuclear bombs detonated in 1945 are the reason why experts can detect fake oil paintings. Isotopes such as strontium-90 and cesium-137 that can be found in oil did not exist in nature before the bombings.

363. Lake Superior has an island, which has a lake, which has an island which has a pond which has a boulder.

364. You are 10 times more likely to get bitten by a New Yorker than a shark.

365. The Darvaza crater, a fiery gas crater in Turkmenistan, is also known as the "Gates of Hell." The origins of the crater is contradictory, but it is believed to have been burning since 1971.

366. There is a feeling similar to deja vu called "deja reve". Deja reve makes you feel like you've previously experienced an event in a dream.

367. The world's fastest land animal was a cheetah called Sarah. At age 11, she ran 100m in 5,95 seconds.

368. Scientists in China have successfully grown teeth out of stem cells found in urine.

369. Honey can't go bad because it's made up of 80% sugar, which helps inhibit the growth of fungi and bacteria and prevents fermentation. It also has antibacterial properties.

370. Natural gas has no odor. Experts add mercaptan to give it its distinctive smell for safety reasons.

371. Strawberries and raspberries aren't really berries in the botanical sense. Botanical berries not commonly known as berries include bananas, tomatoes, grapes, eggplants, persimmons, watermelons, and pumpkins.

372. Apples are made of 23 % air, which is what allows them to float.

373. Some of the people who are born deaf think in sign language. When thinking, they picture themselves using sign language in a first or third person view.

374. The word "orange" was used as the name of the fruit for around 200 years before being known as a color.

375. There are 600,000 pounds of space junk that destroy roughly one satellite per year.

376. The fastest gust of wind ever recorded on Earth was 253 miles per hour.

377. Recent droughts in Europe were the worst in 2,100 years.

378. The best place in the world to see rainbows is in Hawaii. A study published by the American Meteorological Society in 2021 noted that the area's "mountains produce sharp gradients in clouds and rainfall, which are key to abundant rainbow sightings."

379. Mount Everest is bigger now than the last time it was measured. Previous readings have ranged from 29,002 feet above sea level in 1856 down to 20,029 in 1955. After the long process of measuring the mountain with GPS devices, experts have now stated that Mount Everest stands at a whopping 29,031.69 feet.

380. Climate change is causing flowers to change color. A 2020 study led by Clemson University scientists determined that the UV pigmentation in flowers has increased over time which has led to the degradation of their pollen.

381. Dentistry is the oldest profession in the world. One study found evidence of teeth being drilled in skulls that dates from 7,500 to 9,000 years ago.

382. The entire world's population could fit inside Los Angeles. The world's total population is more than 7.5 billion. If every single one of those people stood shoulder-to-shoulder, they could all fit within the 500 square miles of Los Angeles.

383. Four babies are born every second. There are approximately 250 births each minute, 15,000 each hour, and 360,000 each day.

384. The Earth's ozone layer will make a full recovery in 50 years. climate change experts believe that the ozone layer will fully heal within 50 years, according to a 2018 report from the United Nations.

385. People who are currently alive represent about 7% of the total number of people who have ever lived.

SPACE

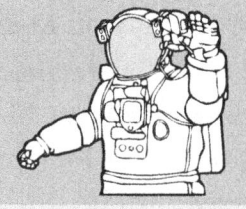

386. Halley's Comet will pass over Earth again on July 26, 2061. The famous comet was last seen on February 9, 1986, and only orbits the Earth once every 75 – 76 years.

387. Mars is the most likely planet in our solar system to be hospitable to life. In 1996, NASA found what they believe may be fossils of microscopic living organisms in a rock recovered from the surface of Mars.

388. In 2006, the International Astronomical Union reclassified Pluto as a dwarf planet. This is because Pluto does not gravitationally dominate the neighborhood around its orbit.

389. There are 5 Dwarf Planets recognized in our Solar System - Ceres, Makemake, Haumea, Eris and Pluto. The dwarf planet Ceres is also the largest asteroid in our solar system.

390. As early as 240BC the Chinese began to document the appearance of Halley's Comet. After 164BC there was a continuous recording of the comet each time it was visible.

391. The center of a comet is called a "nucleus". The streams of dust that streak behind comets are known as a "coma" or a "tail".

392. There are 88 recognized star constellations in our night sky. They cover the Earth's night sky and can be observed from the southern and northern hemispheres.

393. On average it takes the light only 1.3 seconds to travel from the Moon to Earth. The distance between the Earth and the Moon is only 238,855 miles (384,400 kilometers).

394. As space has no gravity, pens won't work. Normal pens work by gravity pulling the ink towards the pen's nib – as you hold the pen in your hand writing part facing downwards.

395. A day on Mercury is equivalent to 58 Earth days.

396. A large percentage of asteroids are pulled in by Jupiter's gravity. Many of the asteroids that are potentially harmful to Earth, the long period comets, tend to be sucked into Jupiter's gravity field.

397. Jupiter's red spot is a huge swirling hurricane-like storm that used to be three times the size of Earth. The storm is shrinking over time, but even as it shrinks it gets taller.

398. Red Dwarf stars that are low in mass can burn continually for up to 10 trillion years.

399. In China, the Milky Way is known as the "Silver River". In Japan and Korea "Silver River" means galaxies in general, not just the Milky Way.

400. Mercury has no atmosphere, which means there is no wind or weather. Instead of an atmosphere, Mercury possesses a thin exosphere made up of atoms blasted off the surface by the solar wind and striking meteoroids.

401. Gennady Padalka currently holds the record for the most days spent in space and he was in orbit for a collective 878 days over the course of five missions

402. "NASA" stands for National Aeronautics and Space Administration. It is an independent agency of the United States Federal Government and was established in 1958.

403. The word "astronaut" means "star sailor" in its origins. It is derived from the Greek words "astron", meaning "star", and "nautes", which means "sailor".

404. A sunset on Mars is blue. The sunsets on Mars appear as blue due to the way the blue light from the Sun is captured within the atmosphere of Mars.

405. Asteroids are the byproducts of formations in the solar system, more than 4 billion years ago.

406. In space suits, there is a small piece of Velcro on the inner part of the helmet that allows astronauts to scratch their nose.

407. Uranus was originally called "George's Star". This name was in honor of discoverer William Hershel's new patron, King George III. The name "Uranus" was proposed in 1782, one year after its discovery, but wasn't officially used until 1850.

408. Saturn is the only planet that could float in water. Saturn is the second largest planet in our solar system, it is also the lightest planet. Saturn could float in water because it is mostly made of gas.

409. The ISS is visible to more than 90% of the Earth's population. When you see the International Space Station (ISS) in the night sky it appears as a fast-moving star crossing from horizon to horizon.

410. The Moon is being pushed away from Earth by 1.6 inches (4 centimeters) per year and our planet's rotation is slowing. Scientists do believe that eventually the Moon will move out of the field of Earth's gravity, however this won't happen for billions of years to come.

411. The center of the Milky Way smells like rum and tastes like raspberries. In 2009, astronomers were able to identify a chemical called ethyl formate in a big dust cloud at the center of the Milky Way. Ethyl formate is responsible for the flavor of raspberries, it also smells like rum.

412. The first artificial satellite in space was called "Sputnik". It was launched by the Soviet Union into an elliptical low Earth orbit on October 4, 1957.

413. The Hubble Space Telescope is one of the most productive scientific instruments ever built. Astronomers using Hubble data have published more than 15,000 scientific papers.

414. The first woman in space was a Russian called Valentina Tereshkova. She launched into space during the Vostok 6 mission on June 16, 1963.

415. Space is completely silent. This is because there is no air in space, and air is needed to carry the sound vibrations.

416. The distance between the Sun and Earth is defined as an Astronomical Unit. An Astronomical Unit (AU) equates to roughly 93 million miles or 150 million kilometers.

417. The first-ever black hole photographed is 3 million times the size of Earth. The photo was released in April 2019 and shows a halo of dust and gas. It was captured by the Event Horizon Telescope, a network of eight linked telescopes.

418. In 2016, scientists detected a radio signal from a source 5 billion light-years away. This means that when the signal started its journey, Earth didn't even exist.

419. Using the naked eye, you can see 3 – 7 different galaxies from Earth. You can see the Andromeda Galaxy (M-31), both Magellanic Clouds, our own Milky Way galaxy, the Triangulum Galaxy (M-33), the Omega Centauri and the Sagittarius Dwarf Spheroidal Galaxy.

420. The Milky Way contains at least one planet per star, resulting in 100–400 billion planets.

421. There are three main types of galaxies: elliptical, spiral and irregular. The Milky Way galaxy is classified as a spiral galaxy.

422. We always see the same side of the Moon, no matter where we stand on Earth. This is because the Moon rotates on its axis at the same rate that it rotates the Earth.

423. The International Space Station circles Earth every 92 minutes. The speed of the ISS is roughly 17,150 miles per hour.

424. Outer Space is only 62 miles away. The Kármán line sits at 62 miles above sea-level and is conventionally used as the start of outer space in space treaties and for aerospace records keeping.

425. Any free-moving liquid in outer space will form itself into a sphere. This is because of something called surface tension, which is an imbalance of intermolecular attractive forces.

426. We know more about Mars and our Moon than we do about our oceans. We have fully mapped 100% of the surface of Mars and Earth's Moon, whereas we have only been able to map roughly 5% of the ocean floor.

427. Earth is the only planet not named after a Roman god or goddess, but it is associated with the goddess Terra Mater (Gaea to the Greeks) It is derived from an amalgamation of both the Old English and Old Germanic words for "ground".

428. Because of lower gravity, a person who weighs 220 lbs on Earth would weigh 84 lbs on Mars.

429. The highest mountain discovered is the Olympus Mons, which is located on Mars. Its peak is 16 miles (25 km) high, making it nearly 3 times higher than Mount Everest.

430. Our solar system is 4.6 billion years old. Scientists estimate that in about 5 billion years, our Sun will expand becoming a Red Giant. In about 7.5 billion years its expanding surface will swallow up and engulf the Earth.

431. Even though Mercury is closer to the Sun, Venus is the hottest planet in our solar system. Its thick atmosphere is full of the greenhouse gas carbon dioxide, and it has clouds of sulfuric acid. The atmosphere traps heat, making it feel like a furnace on the surface. The greenhouse effect on Venus causes the temperatures at its surface to reach 864 degrees Fahrenheit (462 degrees Celsius)

432. Mercury and Venus are the only 2 planets in our solar system that have no moons.

433. The Moon is lemon-shaped. Despite its appearance in the night sky, our natural satellite is nowhere near round. The Moon is shaped like a lemon, with flattened poles and bulges on both the near and far side around its equator.

434. Gamma-ray bursts are the strongest and brightest explosions in the universe, thought to be generated during the formation of black holes. The intense radiation of most observed GRBs is thought to be released during a supernova or superluminous supernova as a high-mass star implodes to form a neutron star or a black hole.

435. Gamma-ray bursts can release more energy in 10 seconds than our Sun will in its entire life.

436. Black holes have theoretical opposites known as white holes. A white hole is a bizarre cosmic object which is intensely bright, and from which matter gushes rather than disappears. They are purely hypothetical objects, astronomers are contemplating how they could form in reality.

437. With an average orbital speed of 5.43 km/s, it takes Neptune 164.8 Earth years (60,182 Earth days) to complete a single orbital period. Since it was discovered in 1846, Neptune only recently finished its first full post-discovery orbit in 2011.

438. The Sun loses a billion kilos per second. Particles in the Sun's upper atmosphere are so hot and energetic that they speed out into space as part of the solar wind. Our star sheds around 1.3 trillion trillion trillion particles every second. This equates to roughly one billion kilograms of matter per second, or one Earth every 185 million years.

439. The Carrington Event was the most intense geomagnetic storm in recorded history, occurring on 1–2 September 1859 during solar cycle 10. It created strong auroral displays that were reported globally and caused sparking and fire in multiple telegraph systems. The geomagnetic storm was most likely the result of a coronal mass ejection (CME) from the Sun colliding with Earth's magnetosphere.

440. All of the planets in our solar system can fit in between the earth and the moon. The average Earth-Moon distance is 384,400 km and the total of the planets' average diameters is 380,016 km.

HISTORY

441. The earliest school of medicine was Ayurveda. Charaka is the Father of Ayurveda and after 2500 years, ayurveda is again one of the most famous medications in our civilization.

442. Alexander the Great was buried alive. Alexander's body was paralysed and unresponsive. His body did not decay even after 5 days of his so assumed death. He was thought to be dead and got buried alive.

443. The Sixteenth President of the USA, Abraham Lincoln was declared as a wrestling champ. He was defeated only once in approximately 300 matches.

444. Until the 19th century in Asia, elephants were trained to execute and torture prisoners and traitors.

445. Indian Railways is the world's largest commercial employer, with approximately 1.7 million employees.

446. Albert Einstein, a Jew, but not an Israeli citizen, was once offered the post of Presidency of Israel. He declined, stating that he had "neither the natural ability nor the experience to deal with human beings."

447. Pope Gregory IX said cats were followers of the devil and released a statement to execute them.

448. Yoga's origins can be traced to northern India over 5,000 years ago. Yoga was refined and developed by Rishis (sages) who documented their practices and beliefs in the Upanishads, a huge work containing over 200 scriptures.

449. Nördlingen is a German town built inside a meteor crater. The 25 kilometer-wide Nördlinger Ries crater in which the town sits was formed approximately 15 million years ago after an asteroid collided with this region of Bavaria.

450. In ancient Egypt, pillows were made from many types of hard materials, including ivory, marble, stone, wood, and ceramic. Stone Egyptian headrest pillows were used solely for the dead.

451. The Leaning Tower of Pisa took 344 years to build, beginning in August 1173. It began to lean in 1178 once construction on the second floor had begun. The lean was due to one side sinking into the soft ground.

452. The world's oldest parliament is from Iceland and is called Althing. It was founded in 930 at Thingvellir (the "assembly fields"), which is almost 45 kilometres (28 mi) east of Iceland's capital, Reykjavík.

453. George Washington did not have wooden teeth but he had dentures made of lead, ivory and gold.

454. In the battle of Pelusium, the Persians knew that Egyptians worshipped cats and were forbidden to kill them. So the Persians used them as shields. The Ancient Egyptians were reluctant to kill the cats. They feared the wrath of Goddess Bastet too much. So, they fled the battlefield and lost the Battle of Pelusium in 525 BC.

455. Marie Curie notebooks are radioactive. Her notebooks are still today stored in lead-lined boxes in France, as they were so contaminated with radium, they're radioactive and will be for many years to come.

456. Ancient Egyptian Pharaohs used their workers as fly catchers by covering them with honey so the flies got attached to them.

457. Adolf Hitler's nephew William Patrick Hitler fought against the Nazi in World War II. Adolf Hitler's nephew served in the US Navy in WWII. He serve for three years as a pharmacist's mate receiving a Purple Heart medal for a wound he suffered.

458. The eccentric poet Lord Byron is reported to have kept a bear while he was a student at Trinity College in the early 1800s. He's said to have purchased the bear, quite possibly at Stourbridge Fair, in defiance of the rules that banned students from keeping dogs in college.

459. The knocker-uppers were the human 'alarm clocks'. A knocker-upper, was a member of a profession in Britain and Ireland that started during, and lasted well into, the Industrial Revolution. They were paid to come down the street, usually with a long poles, and tap on the bedroom windows, but some knocker-uppers used a different method. Mary Smith, a famous knocker-upper in London's East End, used shot dried peas out of a pea shooter instead of a pole.

460. Vikings had a settlement in North America exactly one thousand years ago, centuries before Christopher Columbus arrived in the Americas.

461. The sweat of gladiators was thought to be an aphrodisiac. Some ladies even added them into their makeup products.

462. Charlie Chaplin enrolled in a Charlie Chaplin lookalike competition and he came 20th in rank.

463. The Germans and British soldiers paused the war for a day during Christmas Day 1914. They sang, drank and celebrated together. They even had a match of football.

464. One of the earliest known innovators to have created the modern office chair was naturalist Charles Darwin, who put wheels on the chair in his study so he could get to his specimens more quickly.

465. Cleopatra was fluent in 9 languages. They were Ethiopian, Troglodytic, Hebrew, Arabic, Aramaic, Median, Parthian, Egyptian, and Greek.

466. Vladimir Pravik was the first of the few firefighters who reached the Chernobyl Nuclear Power Plant and after the contact to radiation, his eyes turned from brown to blue.

467. Fidel Castro survived 600 assassination attempts.

468. In 1980, IBM produced the first gigabyte-capacity disk drive, the 3380. This hard drive weighed over 500 pounds and had a 2.5GB capacity. It cost $40,000.

469. The country with the most colourful flag in the world is Belize with 12 colours.

470. Adolf Hitler was the first European leader to ban human zoos, a popular attraction in Europe where exotic peoples were paid to be on exhibit for onlookers.

471. Most of the time the Romans did not own cats. Cats were popular in other places but not in Rome. Most of the Roman people had ferrets and the ferrets were kept so that they could keep away the rats and the mice in the area.

472. The first handheld cellular phone call was made on April 3, 1973, by Motorola engineer Martin Cooper from Sixth Avenue in New York while walking between 53rd and 54th streets.

473. The printing press, which revolutionized the sharing of information, was invented by Gutenberg around the year 1440.

474. Egypt is classified as the oldest country in the world, dating back to 3100 BCE.

475. The first web browser, WorldWideWeb, was developed in 1990 by Tim Berners-Lee for the NeXT Computer.

476. The name Sandwich comes from John Montagu, the 4th Earl of Sandwich, an 18th century English aristocrat. He ordered meat tucked into two pieces of bread and others began to order, "the same as Sandwich." Thus, the name was born.

477. "Salvator Mundi" by Leonardo da Vinci is the most expensive painting in the world, valued at $450.3M.

478. The longest reigning monarch ever was Louis XIV of France. He ruled for 72 years, 110 days.

479. King Henry VIII of England had servants called "Grooms of Stool", who wiped him clean after he visited the toilet.

480. The University of Oxford is nearly 700 years older than the USA, 400 years older than the English Language, 300 years older than Machu Picchu, 200 years older than Aztecs and 150 years older than Easter Island heads. There is no clear date of foundation, but teaching existed at Oxford in some form in 1096 and developed rapidly from 1167.

481. The first airplane flight was only 65 years before the moon landing. Wright Brothers' first flight was December 17, 1903 and Apollo 11 was July 16-24, 1969, roughly 65.5 years between the two events.

482. George Washington opened a whiskey distillery after his presidency. After his term, Washington opened a whiskey distillery. By 1799, Washington's distillery was the largest in the country, producing 11,000 gallons of unaged whiskey.

483. During the Salem witch trials, the accused witches weren't actually burned at the stake. Twenty people were eventually executed as witches, but contrary to popular belief, none of the condemned was burned at the stake. In accordance with English law, 19 of the victims of the Salem Witch Trials were instead taken to the infamous Gallows Hill to die by hanging.

484. President Zachary Taylor died from a cherry overdose. Zachary Taylor passed away after eating way too many cherries and drinking milk at a Fourth of July party in 1850. He died on July 9th from gastroenteritis.

485. The Bloody Mary wasn't always called Bloody Mary. First, the popular brunch drink was actually called A Bucket Of Blood. After Bucket Of Blood, it transitioned to Red Snapper and, finally, settled on Bloody Mary.

486. In the Ancient Olympics, athletes performed naked. This was to achieve closeness to the gods and also help detox their skin through sweating. The word "gymnastics" comes from the Ancient Greek words "gumnasía" ("athletic training, exercise") and "gumnós" ("naked").

487. Andrew Jackson had a pet parrot. And he taught his parrot, Polly, to curse like a sailor. Andrew Jackson's African Grey parrot was removed from his funeral at The Hermitage, Tennessee, for swearing so loud and long it disturbed the attendees.

488. The ancient Romans often used stale urine as mouthwash. The main ingredient in urine is ammonia which acts as a powerful cleaning agent.

489. In 1386, a pig was executed in France. In the Middle Ages, a pig attacked a child who went to die later from their wounds. The pig was arrested, kept in prison, and then sent to court where it stood trial for murder, was found guilty and then executed by hanging.

490. During the Great Depression, people made clothes out of food sacks. People used flour bags, potato sacks, and anything made out of burlap. Because of this trend, food distributors started to make their sacks more colorful to help people remain a little bit fashionable.

491. Russia ran out of vodka celebrating the end of World War II. When the long war ended, street parties engulfed the Soviet Union, lasting for days–until all of the nation's vodka reserves ran out.

492. In 18th century England, pineapples were a status symbol. Those rich enough to own a pineapple would carry them around to signify their personal wealth and high-class status. Pineapples would often be depicted in commissioned paintings or it would be featured in wooden furniture.

493. Ancient Greeks Believed That Redheads Turned Into Vampires After They Died. They burned their bodies to stop them from rising from the grave.

494. Roman gladiators often became celebrities and even endorsed products. Children would play with gladiator 'action figures' made out of clay.

495. Cars weren't invented in the United States. The first car was created in the 19th century when European engineers Karl Benz and Emile Levassor were working on automobile inventions. Benz patented the first automobile in 1886.

496. Abraham Lincoln was also a licensed bartender. In 1833, the 16th president opened up a bar called Berry and Lincoln with his friend William F. Berry in New Salem, Illinois.

497. Roman Catholics in Bavaria founded a secret society in 1740 called the Order of the Pug. New members had to wear dog collars and scratch at the door to get in. This para-Masonic society was reportedly active until 1902.

498. Between the 11th and 19th centuries, a number of Buddhist monks successfully mummified themselves. They adopted a practice called Sokushinbutsu in which they gradually weaned themselves off food and water and essentially starved themselves to death over the course of a thousand days.

499. The Luftwaffe had a master interrogator, Hanns Scharff, whose tactic was being as nice as possible. Scharff's best tactics for getting information out of prisoners included: nature walks without guards present, baking them homemade food, cracking jokes, drinking beers, and afternoon tea with German fighter aces.

500. Back in the 16th century, the wealthy elite used to eat dead bodies. It was rumored the cadavers could cure diseases. Egyptian mummies was the highest delicacy.

501. 100 million years ago, the Sahara Desert was inhabited by galloping crocodiles. Back then, the Sahara Desert was a lush oasis full of life and full of predators. In 2009, fossil hunters found the remains of crocodiles that had large land-going legs.

502. Before the 19th century, dentures were made from dead soldiers' teeth. After the Battle of Waterloo, dentists ran to the battlefield to seek out teeth from the thousands of dead soldiers.

503. Roman Emperor Gaius, also known as Caligula, made one of his favorite horses a senator. The emperor loved his horse, named Incitatus, so much that he gave him a marble stall, an ivory manger, a jeweled collar, and even a house.

504. When Louis XVI and Marie Antoinette were beheaded, it is said that people dipped handkerchiefs in their blood to keep as souvenirs. In 2011, a group of scientists confirmed that a blood-stained handkerchief dated from approximately 1793 was soaked in the blood of Louis XVI.

505. Joan of Arc said that she received visions of the archangel Michael, Saint Margaret, and Saint Catherine of Alexandria instructing her to support Charles VII and recover France from English domination late in the Hundred Years' War.

506. Joan of Arc convinced Charles VII she could lead his armies with no experience. She routed the English, survived a 60-foot escape leap from a tower uninjured, was falsely accused of heresy, and burned at the stake, all between the ages of 17 and 19. She was guided by voices only she could hear.

507. The sound made by the Krakatoa volcanic eruption in 1883 was so loud it ruptured eardrums of people 40 miles away, traveled around the world four times, and was clearly heard 3,000 miles away.

508. The Tale of Two Lovers written in 1444 was one of the bestselling books of the fifteenth century, even before its author, Aeneas Sylvius Piccolomini, became Pope Pius II. It is one of the earliest examples of an epistolary novel, full of erotic imagery.

509. It's believed that roughly 97% of history has been lost over time. Written accounts of history only started roughly 6,000 years ago. And modern humans first appeared around 200,000 years ago.

510. During World War II, Americans called hamburgers "liberty steaks". This was because "hamburger" sounded a little too German. Also, during World War II, sauerkraut was re-dubbed "liberty cabbage".

511. There were "dance marathons" during the Great Depression. These human endurance contests served as a way of giving financially unstable married couples a roof over their head and food to eat for a few days.

512. One in 200 men are direct descendants of Genghis Khan. The Mongolian Emperor was known for siring at least 11 children. Scientists conducted a study in 2003 which showed that one in 200 men share a Y chromosome with the conqueror.

513. Julius Caesar added three extra intercalary months to recalibrate the calendar in preparation for his calendar reform, which went into effect in 45 BC. This year therefore had 445 days, and was nicknamed the annus confusionis ("year of confusion") and serves as the longest recorded calendar year in human history.

514. Back in Colonial America, slaves could win their freedom through lawsuits. Although there was a low chance of succeeding, winning in court meant that the slave was now a citizen. Since slaves often didn't have last names and needed a last name to be a citizen, they were often just given the last name of 'Freeman'.

515. Alexander the Great named over 70 cities after himself. Alexander the Great conquered over 2 million square miles of the Earth's surface all by the time he was 30.

516. Paul Tibbets, pilot of the Enola Gay the plane that dropped the first nuclear bomb on Hiroshima, didn't have a funeral or headstone. Tibbets decided he didn't want a funeral or a headstone as he worried it would become a place for protesting nuclear armament. Instead, he was cremated and his ashes were scattered over the English Channel.

517. Shakespeare originated the "yo momma" joke. In his play, Titus Andronicus, one of the characters, Chiron, exclaims "Thou has undone our mother" to which another character, Aaron, replies "Villain, I have done thy mother."

518. The Circus Maximum in Rome is still the largest capacity sports arena ever built. It was used for the execution of prisoners, part of the Roman Triumph, and chariot racing. Historians believe the Circus Maximum could hold between 150,000 – 250,000 people at any given time.

519. Spartans were so rich that nobody had to work. Ancient Sparta was an immensely wealthy country. Mainly due to their conquest and domination of their neighbors, the Helots.

520. During a Roman Triumph, soldiers sang lewd songs about their commanders to amuse the crowds.

521. Since the end of WWI, over 1,000 people have died from leftover unexploded bombs.

522. Thomas Edison didn't invent most of the stuff he patented. Of the 1,093 things he put a patent on, he stole most of them off geniuses like Nikola Tesla, Wilhelm Rontgen, and Joseph Swan - who originally invented the lightbulb.

523. Turkeys were once worshiped as Gods. The Mayan people believed turkeys were the vessels of the Gods and honored them with worship.

524. Fox Tossing was once a popular sport. Popular with Europe's elite during the 17th and 18th centuries, fox tossing would involve a person throwing a fox as far and as high as they could.

525. The saying "fly off the handle" originates from the 1800s. It's a saying that refers to cheap axe-heads flying off their handles when swung backward before a chop.

526. 4% of the Normandy beaches are made up of shrapnel from the D-Day Landings. More than 5,000 tons of bombs were dropped by the Allies on the Axis powers as part of the prelude to the Normandy landings.

527. An ancient text called the Voynich Manuscript still baffles scientists. Hand-written in an unknown language, the Voynich Manuscript has been carbon-dated to roughly 1404 – 1438. Hundreds of cryptographers and master codebreakers have tried to decipher it over the years with none succeeding to grasp its meaning or origin.

528. Since 1945, all British tanks are equipped with tea-making facilities.

529. In Ancient Greece, wearing skirts was manly. Greeks viewed trousers as effeminate and would mock any men who wore them.

530. America's National School Lunch Program of 1946 was due to WWII. This is due to the fact that the government realized by giving the children free meals, they would have a healthier draft pool if they ever needed it again.

531. The first official Medals of Honor were awarded during the American Civil War. They were awarded to Union soldiers who participated in the Great Locomotive Chase of 1862.

532. On January 1, 1892, Annie Moore was the first passenger to disembark at Ellis Island on its opening day. She had traveled to the United States with her two younger brothers aboard the SS Nevada after departing from Queenstown, Ireland.

533. The first time the word "period" was used on TV in reference to menstruation was 1985.

534. A singing birthday card has more computer power in it than the entire Allied Army of WWII.

535. Augustus Caesar was the wealthiest man to ever live in history. Nephew and heir of Julius Caesar, Roman Emperor Augustus had an estimated net worth of $.46 trillion when counting for inflation.

536. The world's most successful pirate in history was a lady. Named Ching Shih, she was a prostitute in China. This was until the Commander of the Red Flag Fleet bought and married her. But rather than just viewing her as a wife, her husband considered her his equal and she became an active pirate commander in the fleet. Under Shih's leadership, the Red Flag Fleet consisted of over 300 warships, with a possible 1,200 more support ships.

537. The UK government collected postcards as intelligence for the D-Day landings. This was an intelligence-gathering exercise. Initiated by Lieutenant General Frederick Morgan, he was searching for the hardest beaches to defend.

538. Germany uncovers 2,000 tons of unexploded bombs every year. Over the course of WWII, the Allied armies dropped roughly 2.7 million tons of bombs over Nazi-occupied Europe. Half of that landed on Germany.

539. Tug of War used to be an Olympic sport. It was part of the Olympic schedule between 1900 and 1920 and occurred at 5 Olympic Games.

540. During the Victorian period, it was normal to photograph relatives after they died. People would dress their newly-deceased relatives in their best clothing, and then put them in lifelike poses and photograph them.

541. People were buried alive so often, that bells were attached to their coffins. Due to medicine not being so great, comatose people were sometimes mistakenly buried alive. In order to counteract these potential blunders, people were buried with little bells above ground. These bells were attached to a string, which went into the coffin.

542. The term "saved by the bell" does not originate from people being buried alive. It comes from being saved from a knockout or countdown by the ring of a bell, which signals the end of the current round.

543. In the Victorian era, men with mustaches used special cups. Pragmatically called "mustache cups", these specially-made mugs had guards on them which prevented a man's mustache from dipping into their warm cup of tea.

544. Spartan women-owned most of the land and wealth in Sparta. When a Spartan man died, his public state-given farmland went back to the state. However, his private land would go to his wife.

545. For 12 years during the French Revolutionary Period, France had a whole new calendar. Between 1793 and 1805, the ruling French government used the French Republican Calendar to remove all religious and royalist ties to the old calendar. It was also part of a wider effort to decimalize France in terms of time, currency and metrication. The French Republican Calendar had 10-hour days, with 100 minutes to an hour, and 100 seconds to a minute.

546. Genghis Khan created one of the first international postal systems. One of his earliest decrees as Khan was to establish a mounted courier service called the "Yam". The "Yam" grew into a military postal service spanning across multiple borders, complete with a network of post houses and waystations across the whole of his Empire.

MUSIC

547. "Hurrian Hymn No. 6" is considered the world's earliest melody, but the oldest musical composition to have survived in its entirety is a first century A.D. Greek tune known as the "Seikilos Epitaph." The song was found engraved on an ancient marble column used to mark a woman's gravesite in Turkey. The lyrics read, "While you live, shine. Have no grief at all. Life exists for only a short while. And time demands his due."

548. The world's largest performing rock band included 953 musicians. The Beijing Contemporary Music Academy achieved this record on June 16, 2016. They performed in the city of Tianjin, China. The band included 349 singers, 154 guitarists, and 151 drummers. 100 bassists also took part in the performance, along with 100 keyboard players, and 98 players of wind instruments.

549. Simon Desorgher assembled the most number of chimes as a single musical instrument. Also known as tubular bells, Simon Desorgher's instrument included 120 aluminum tubes.

550. David Stanley and The Music Man Project assembled the world's biggest triangle ensemble. The ensemble included 1,521 players on October 15, 2017. They performed as part of the London Palladium's Music is Magic concert.

551. Japan has the shortest national anthem in the world. Japan's national anthem "Kimi Ga Yo" has only four lines. This gives it the record for the shortest national anthem in the world.

552. Hans Zimmer does not have a formal background in music - his only formal study in music was piano lessons as a child.

553. Thomas Dorsey is the Father of Gospel Music. He made his career writing and performing secular music. After his wife's death in 1931, he switched genres to gospel music.

554. The song 4'33" is only silence. Composer John Cage released the song in 1952. The name references its length of 4 minutes and 33 seconds. At that time, none of the orchestra would play their instruments. Instead, the audience would listen only to the sounds of their surroundings. John Cage called it proof of the idea that any sound could be music.

555. Archaeological evidence shows China's musical tradition going back to 3000 BC.

556. Japanese comedian Pikotaro released "Pen-Pineapple-Apple-Pen" in 2016. It gained 1 million hits on the internet and a place in USA's Billboard Hot 100 charts. At 45 seconds long, it broke the record for the shortest song on the chart.

557. The cheapest a CD will get in Japan is $25. People still buy a lot of CDs in Japan. 85% of all music sales in Japan are from CD purchases.

558. Elvis Presley was once told he had no talent. Elvis Presley's first stage performance at the Grand Ole Opry in Tennessee failed to impress. This led talent manager Jim Denny to tell Elvis to go back to driving trucks.

559. ABBA comes from the names of the band's members. Agnetha Fältskog, Björn Ulvaeus, Benny Andersson, and Anni-Frid Lyngstad make up the band.

560. Led Zeppelin was recording a new single when a black dog walked into their studio. That song was later released with the name Black Dog.

561. The Beatles sang the song "Got to Get You into My Life" in 1966. They released it as part of the album "Revolver." Paul McCartney admitted in 1997 that the 'you' in the song's title referred to Marijuana.

562. Madonna's career goes back to before she started singing. In the 1970s, she was a drummer for the band Breakfast Club.

563. The origins of the word Jazz are not known.

564. While music is an effective means of treatment, it's best used with others. One example is for therapists working with troubled youth. Active musical therapy has helped build trust from the patient to the therapist.

565. Jazz inspired the word hipster. The root of hipster is hep, 1930s slang for someone considered fashionable. Those included jazz players, and from there developed to hipster.

566. Studies show that jazz music stimulates the brain into producing Theta brainwaves. These brain waves are usually most active during problem solving and creative activities. Jazz's rhythms are also known to reduce anxiety and stress the same way a massage does.

567. The most common instruments in jazz are what's called the Piano Trio. A piano trio includes a piano, a bass, and drums.

568. Nonverbal signals are common in jazz performances. These signals take many forms, from nods of the head to subtle pointing of an instrument. They are usually used to signal the beginning and end of performances.

569. Country music is now a global phenomenon. Country music is usually associated with the American countryside. But, the styles and themes of country music have since spread around the world.

570. The Day the Music Died refers to two plane crashes that killed musicians aboard. The first Day that Music Died was on February 3, 1959. A plane crash in Ohio killed musicians Buddy Holly, Ritchie Valens, and the Big Bopper. The second was in 1963, involving a plane crash in Tennessee. Killed aboard were Patsy Cline, Hawkshaw Hawkins, and Cowboy Copas.

571. Bluegrass country music comes from Kentucky, USA. In the 1930s, musicians in Kentucky experimented with Celtic fiddles and modern styles. The result was what's now known as Bluegrass country music. One of the greatest bluegrass artists was Bill Monroe and his band The Bluegrass Boys.

572. Karaoke means empty orchestra. The Japanese word karaoke comes from two other words. Karappo, which means empty in Japanese, and okesutura, the Japanized form of orchestra.

573. Havergal Brian's Gothic symphony requires a thousand performers. Out of the 1,000, 800 are singers, and the remaining 200 make up the orchestra.

574. Mozart has a chocolate brand named after him. Called Mozartkugel or Mozart ball, they were first sold by Paul Fürst in 1890. They are handmade and have Mozart's images shown on the wrapper. They remain in the market today and are very popular in Austria.

575. In 1987, Aretha Franklin became the first woman to be inducted into the Rock and Roll Hall of Fame.

576. With a net worth of 1.3 billion dollars, Paul McCartney is the wealthiest musician in the world.

577. In 2013, Metallica became the first band to play a concert on every continent on Earth.

578. LeAnn Rimes won a Grammy award when she was just 14 years old, making her the youngest person to receive this award. She won for her 1997 remake of Blue, originally recorded by Bill Mack in 1958.

579. With more than 250 million recordings sold, The Beatles are the all-time best selling band in the world.

580. When Pope John Paul II visited Canada in 1984, Celine Dion performed Une Colombe during his appearance at the Olympic stadium in Montreal. There were 60,000 people in the audience.

581. Elvis Presley played 636 consecutive shows in Las Vegas over an eight-year period (1969-1976). He played two shows per evening every day of the week. Each show sold out.

582. MTV, the first TV channel dedicated to playing music videos 24/7, launched on August 1, 1981. The first video played on MTV was for the song Video Killed the Radio Star by The Buggles.

583. In 1985, the Live Aid music festival organized by Bob Geldof raised $127 million for Ethiopian famine relief. Live Aid aired on TV around the world, showing live performances from London and Philadelphia.

584. Composer John Williams has received over 50 Oscar nominations and has won more Oscars than any other living composer. His first Oscar was for the score of Fiddler on the Roof in 1972.

585. The last episode of the long-running Seinfeld sitcom concluded with the Green Day song Time of Your Life.

586. Over half of the households in the U.S. have at least one person who plays one or more musical instruments.

587. In 1967, entrepreneur Shigeichi Negishi invented what he called the Sparko Box. This device is the very first known karaoke machine.

588. Listening to music that you enjoy can help you relax and relieve stress. Slower tempos seem to be best for quieting a busy mind and relaxing tense muscles.

589. Paul and Joseph Galvin introduced the first in-car radios in the early 1930s. They combined the word motor (for car) with Victrola (for music player) to come up with the name Motorola for their innovation.

590. Approximately 90% of social media users engage in some kind of music-related activity via their apps and profiles. Activities include things like engaging with artists or using song lyrics as image captions.

591. Listening to music at bedtime helps many people (children and adults alike) fall asleep faster.

592. There are five kinds of musical instruments. Percussion instruments are struck. String instruments have their strings strummed. Both woodwind and brass instruments get blown. Keyboard instruments have their keys pressed.

593. The record for the world's longest marathon drumming by an entire team is 3 days, 8 hours, and 2 minutes.

594. There are 8 notes in music. In most countries, they're read as Do-Re-Mi-Fa-Sol-La-Si. In Britain and Holland, they are instead substituted with the first 7 letters of the alphabet. The eighth note is always called the octave.

595. Music began to step away from religion in the Renaissance. The printing press made it easier to produce and spread musical compositions. This was unlike the Middle Ages, where everything was handmade. The Renaissance also saw the rise of Humanism, under its influence, musicians experimented with new instruments and styles.

596. Adelina Patti was an opera singer from the late 19th century. During a performance at London's Covent Garden in 1895, she wore a costume worth £15 million. It was and remains to be the most expensive opera costume of all time.

597. Mozart sold the most CDs in 2016, beating out Adele, Drake, and Beyoncé, even though all of those artists had Grammy-winning hits that year.

598. Multiple studies have been conducted that prove singing as a part of a group provides numerous physical and emotional benefits. When you sing with others, the body releases feel-good hormones, like oxytocin, and reduces stress-causing ones, like cortisol.

599. Research has consistently shown that the synchronization of music with repetitive exercise provides enhanced physical performance, helping people both work out for longer and train more efficiently.

600. Rod Stewart's 1993 New Year's Eve concert on Copacabana Beach in Rio de Janeiro, Brazil, remains the most-attended free concert that ever took place. An estimated 4.2 million people were in attendance at this performance.

601. In 2014, a group of researchers released an online test called "Hooked on Music." They found that "Wannabe" by The Spice Girls was the catchiest song - people were able to recognize it in about 2.3 seconds, which was way below the 5-second average of identifying other popular songs.

602. Finland Has the Most Metal Bands Per Capita. Finland is home to the most bands of this genre, with 53.5 metal bands per 100,000 people. Second place is tied between two other Nordic nations Sweden and Norway - 27.2 metal bands.

603. In 2015, a Canadian astronaut named Chris Hadfield released his first album, which was entirely recorded while he was in orbit. Not only was he the first Canadian to walk in space, he's also a talented musician who went viral with a cover of David Bowie's "Space Oddity."

604. According to reports, British naval officers play Britney Spears songs to scare away Somali pirates off of Africa's eastern coast. Her songs "Oops I Did It Again" and "Baby One More Time" are the songs which are used.

605. "Jingle Bells" is a Christmas classic, but it didn't originate that way. Written by James Lord Pierpont and published in 1857, it was meant to be sung during Thanksgiving.

606. A study conducted by South Korean scientists from the National Institute of Agricultural Biotechnology found that plants grow faster when music is played around them.

607. The Most Expensive Musical Instrument Sold for $15.9 Million. In 2011, the "Lady Blunt" Stradivarius violin sold for a world record $15.9 million, which was four times the previous auction record for a Stradivarius.

608. Students who have experience with music performance or taking music appreciation courses score higher on the SAT. One report indicated that they score, on average, 63 points higher on verbal and 44 points higher on math.

609. The World's Longest Running Performance will end in the 27th Century. A 639-year performance based on avant-garde composer John Cage's "As Slow as Possible" started in September 2001 and is still running at St. Buchard Church in Germany. The performance by an automated organ progresses so slowly that visitors have to wait months for a chord change, and is scheduled to conclude in 2640.

610. None of The Beatles Could Read or Write Music.

611. A study conducted at the University of Pavia in Italy showed that music promotes a healthy cardiovascular system by triggering physiological changes that modulate blood pressure, heart rate, and respiratory functions.

612. International Strange Music Day (August 24th) was created by a New York City musician named Patrick Grant, to encourage people to play and listen to new types of music they're not familiar with or appreciate music you might otherwise consider to be strange or bizarre.

613. The Sea Organ is located on the shores of Zadar, Croatia, and is the world's first musical pipe organs that is played by the sea. Steps carved in white stone were built on the quayside. Underneath, there are 35 musically tuned tubes with whistle openings on the sidewalk. The movement of the sea pushes air through, and depending on the size and velocity of the wave – musical chords are played.

614. In 2008, a French study found that loud music in a bar setting leads to more drinking in less time.

615. Heavy Metal and Classical Music Fans Have Similar Personality Traits. The findings came from research conducted by Heriot-Watt University in Scotland, which examined the personalities of more than 36,000 music fans from all over the world. Both groups tend to be creative, at ease with themselves, and introverted.

616. Monaco's army has just 82 soldiers. Its military orchestra has 85 musicians. This makes Monaco the only country whose army is smaller than its military orchestra.

617. "Born in the USA" isn't pro-American. Bruce Springsteen wrote "Born in the USA" about his anger towards the country's treatment of Vietnam vets. The song was misinterpreted by many, even by President Regan, who used it during his 1984 re-election campaign.

618. Prince Played 27 Instruments on His Debut Album.

TECHNOLOGY

619. Phantom vibration syndrome or phantom ringing syndrome is the perception that one's mobile phone is vibrating or ringing when it is not.

620. Instead of mowing their lawn, Google rents goats to eat the grass at their Mountain View headquarters. A herder will bring 200 goats which are herded by a border collie named Jen.

621. The etymology of "robot," comes from the Czech word "robota" which translates to forced labor or work. The word was first used to refer to a fictional humanoid in a play in 1920.

622. When the first VCR (Video Camera Recorder) was made in 1956, it was the size of a piano.

623. Domain name registration used to be free. Registering a domain name was free until 1995.

624. Megabytes used to weigh hundreds of pounds. In 1956, the first computer had something similar to a hard drive. The cabinet that contained the hard drive weighed over 2,200 pounds and could hold 5 MBs of data.

625. The Radio took 38 years to reach an audience of 50 million.

626. The first photograph ever taken in 1826 took 8 hours to expose. The world's first photograph was taken by Joseph Nicéphore Niépce in 1826 or 1827. Captured using a technique known as heliography, the shot was taken from an upstairs window at Niépce's estate in Burgundy. Louis Daguerre, was able to lower that time to just 15 minutes in 1839.

627. People read faster or slower depending on what they read from. On average, people read 10% slower from a screen than from paper.

628. Even though it is free to use GPS globally, it costs $2 million dollars to operate every day.

629. There are computers specially designed without internet, video, or music capabilities, just for the Amish. The features include word processing, drawing, accounting, spreadsheets and more.

630. In 1964, Douglas Engelbart invented the first-ever computer mouse. It was made out of wood. It was rectangular and featured a little button on the top right. He called it a mouse because the cord coming out of the back reminded him of the tiny rodents.

631. Email spam, also referred to as junk email, is unsolicited messages sent in bulk by email (spamming). The name comes from a Monty Python sketch in which the name of the canned pork product Spam is ubiquitous, unavoidable, and repetitive.

632. Invented by Levi Hutchins in 1787, the first mechanical alarm clock could only ring at 4 a.m. (in order to wake him for his job) The French inventor Antoine Redier was the first person to patent an adjustable mechanical alarm clock, in 1847. On October 24, 1876, a mechanical wind-up alarm clock that could be set for any time was patented by Seth E Thomas.

633. Computer Security Day is celebrated on November 30th. It was started in 1988 to help raise awareness of computer-related security issues.

634. In November 2010 the Air Force Research Laboratory created a powerful supercomputer, nicknamed the "Condor Cluster," by connecting together 1,760 PlayStation 3 consoles which include 168 separate graphical processing units and 84 coordinating servers in a parallel array capable of performing 500 trillion floating-point operations.

635. The first product scanned was a packet of chewing gum in 1974. Norman Joseph Woodland invented the barcode and received a patent in October 1952.

636. Surgeons that grew up playing video games more than 3 hours per week make 37% fewer errors. They also had a 27% faster completion rate when it comes to performing laparoscopic surgery, as well as suturing.

637. Apollo 11 astronauts couldn't afford insurance. Life insurance for a space mission cost a fortune because the risks were extremely high back then. As a backup, each of them had autographed hundreds of their posters. So, if they do not make it back then their families could sell these to collectors to fund their kids' college tuition.

638. 220 million tons of old computers, along with other devices, are thrown away every year in the U.S. alone.

639. The European Union is suggesting laws that implement an emergency kill switch into all robots. Also, they will be required to be programmed to never harm a human.

640. Most of the purchases in China are done with mobile phones. Around 70% of online purchases are made with mobile phones. Only 46% of online purchases in the U.S. are done with a cell phone.

641. Between adult users in the Philippines, 93% use social networking sites, which is higher than the 74% that use it in the U.S.

642. There are only 21 million Bitcoins that can be mined in total. Only 10% of Bitcoin's 21 Million Supply is left to be mined.

643. The first computer virus was harmless. In 1971, the first ever computer virus was developed. Named Creeper, it was made as an experiment just to see how it spread between computers. The virus simply displayed the message: "I'm the creeper, catch me if you can!"

644. Google uses about 2.26 million megawatt hours per year to power its global data center operations, which is equivalent to the power necessary to sustain 200,000 homes.

645. It is estimated that digital technology could reduce global carbon emissions by 20% by 2030.

646. An artificial intelligence was created (with 87% accuracy) in determining disease outbreaks, such as dengue fever. There are hopes to use this tech to predict outbreaks for more serious diseases like Ebola and Zika.

647. There is a machine that can predict heart attacks. It can predict heart attacks up to four hours before they happened – with 80% accuracy.

648. Digital music sales surpassed physical sales in 2014. In 2014, the download sales and subscriptions made $6.85 billion, while physical sales were under it at $6.82 billion.

649. The top three most used passwords are 123456, password, and 12345. They are also the weakest.

650. CAPTCHA is a long acronym, it stands for "Completely Automatic Public Turning Test to Tell Computers and Humans Apart".

651. About 51% of internet traffic is non-human. Over 30% is from hacking programs, spammers, and phishing.

652. Most of today's successful companies started in garages.

653. An average 21 year old has spent 5,000 hours playing video games.

654. Every advertisement for iPhone's have 9:41 set as the time. In 2007, Steve Jobs first announced the iPhone at that time. The first photo of the iPhone showed the time 9:41, at exactly 9:41am.

655. On 18 July, 1992 – the first picture was uploaded on the web. The photo that captured four women was posted by Tim Berners-Lee, the inventor of the World Wide Web. The four women belonged to an all-female comedy band called Les Horrible Cernettes

656. Until 2010, carrier pigeons were faster than the internet. A test was done to fly a carrier pigeon with a USB stick 50 miles to an internet provider, while racing against an internet upload. The pigeon made it in just over an hour, while the upload took over two hours.

657. Tech companies often test their products in New Zealand. The main reason is that since it's somewhat isolated, news about a product failing won't spread very fast.

658. There's a term for old people who use the internet. Silver surfer refers to the population of individuals over the age of 50 who utilize the internet on a consistent basis.

659. Technical degrees are almost useless by the time you graduate. The amount of technical information doubles every two years. If you start a four year degree, then half of what you learn by the time you finish will be obsolete.

660. The world spends about 164 million hours every day streaming Netflix, which is equivalent to 18,812 years' worth of TV and movies every 24 hours.

661. Over 90% of the world's currency is digital. This means that most of the money in credit cards, debit cards, direct deposit, and online purchases exist on computers and hard drives, leaving only about 8% of global currency as physical money.

662. The password for the nuclear missiles were just a string of zero's. For 20 years, the password was eight zero's all in a row, and it was written down so nobody forgot.

663. Nigeria, Ghana, and Bangladesh - less than 1% of residents in these countries have a landline, but over 85% have access to cell phones.

664. The first webpage is still running. In 1991, Tim Berners-Lee was working on developing the World Wide Web. That page is still up and functioning at info.cern.ch

665. When typewriters were introduced, typing too fast would jam the keys. Using a QWERTY keyboard spaced out commonly used characters to slow typists down and prevent jamming.

666. In 1999, Gran Turismo 2, the 2-disc edition of the game, the blue disc featured the smell of fuel and burning rubber. When FIFA 2001 was released in 2000, they used Scratch and Sniff technology on their discs so it smelled like football stadium turf.

667. The word "Android" literally means a human with a male robot appearance. The female equivalent of this word is a "Gynoid."

668. Samuel F.B. Morse developed an electric telegraph (1832–35) and then invented, with his friend Alfred Vail, the Morse Code (1838). The latter is a system for representing letters of the alphabet, numerals, and punctuation marks by arranging dots, dashes, and spaces.

669. In 2004, the @ symbol became the first new character to be added to Morse code for the first time in many decades. The character is called a "Commat," and consists of the signals for A and C with no break in between.

670. 97% of people type in words to Google just to see if they spelled it right.

671. There are over 35 billion Google searches each month.

672. In 2012, at least six girls were named Apple, 49 boys were named Mac, and at least 17 girls were named Siri. Alexa was the 32nd most popular name for girls born in 2015 but dropped to 90th place in 2018.

673. There is special Braille technology and accessories for blind people to use cell phones. It uses special pins that go up and down so the user can touch and read the info.

674. Google's first-ever Tweet on Twitter was in February 2009, and reads - "I'm 01100110 01100101 01100101 01101100 01101001 01101110 01100111 00100000 01101100 01110101 01100011 01101011 01111001 00001010." Translating from binary into English, this tweet says "I'm feeling lucky."

675. The first text message was transmitted Dec. 3, 1992. Engineer Neil Papworth typed "merry Christmas" on a computer and sent the first SMS message to the cellphone of Vodafone director Richard Jarvis.

676. Over 6,000 new computer viruses are created and released every month. Today, 90% of emails contain some form of malware and most people don't know about it.

677. NASA's internet speed is 91 GB per second. The average household internet speeds are roughly 25 MB per second.

678. Every day, over 300 million photos are uploaded to Facebook, while 800 million likes are given out per day.

679. Nokia is the largest company from Finland. This brand was originally a paper manufacturer in 1865. Nokia branched out into technology in the 1980s.

680. Out of all the 7.7 billion people in the world, over 6 billion of those have access to a cell phone. Only 4.5 billion have access to working toilets

681. The Apple Lisa was the first commercial computer with a Graphical User Interface (GUI) and a mouse. The Lisa was first introduced in January 19, 1983 at a cost of $9,995.

682. Technophobia, (not an officially recognized mental illness), is the extreme and irrational fear of technology. This fear is related to an irrational fear of computers, robots, artificial intelligence, weapons, and other such objects.

683. In 2006, Qatar Telecom hosted a charity auction where they sold the phone number 666-6666. It sold for $2.75 million, bought by an anonymous bidder.

684. Mark Zuckerberg is color blind. The founder of Facebook purposely chose a blue color scheme because he has red-green color blindness.

685. 40% of couples who got together in 2017 met online, and meeting through friends declined by 13% from 1995 to 2017.

686. The music category received 20% of all total views on YouTube last year — but makes up only 5% of YouTube's total content.

687. Facebook pays $500 for reporting any vulnerability in their security.

688. Studies have shown that the more time kids spend on social media, the less likely they are to be happy with their overall life by 14%.

689. The average adult will spend over 10 hours online every day, with around 2.5 of those hours being spent on social media.

690. The highest internet speed can be found in Taiwan, with an average of 85.02 Mbps (megabits per second). The country with the slowest is Yemen, which has an average speed of just 0.38 Mbps.

691. The distribution of information using technology has been explored since the 1900s. But it wasn't until the '60s that the 'Intergalactic Network' was created, followed very shortly by the ARPNET or 'Advanced Research Projects Agency Network'.

692. In 1965 an experiment took place at the MIT Lincoln Lab. The experiment was a success, for the first time ever two computers communicated with each other.

693. On March 26, 1976, the Queen of England sent her first email. Queen Elizabeth II took part in a demonstration to showcase this new technology.

694. Ethernet was invented in the early '70s, by Robert Metcalfe. This still is the most commonly used way to connect to the internet using wires.

695. The first option for commercial internet use was known as dial-up. Dial-up required a phone line for connection, meaning that the landline couldn't be used while the internet was in use.

696. Dial-up was incredibly slow, downloading a file could take hours, and streaming music or a film was virtually impossible. The best connection available in '95 was 56kbps.

697. In the early 2000s, broadband started to replace dial-up. This method allowed higher volumes of data to be transferred faster, using something called an ADSL, Asymmetric Digital Subscriber Line connection.

698. Wireless internet was founded in September 1990, but it wasn't available commercially until 1999.

699. The definition of what we now know as Wi-Fi is: 'wireless networking technology that uses radio waves to provide high-speed network and Internet connections'.

700. Some of the other names considered for this new technology were: WaveLAN, FlankSpeed, DragonFly, WECA and the IEEE 802.11b Direct Sequence.

701. A company named Interbrand suggested the term Wi-Fi as a play on 'High Fidelity'. High fidelity is a high quality reproduction of sound. So 'Hi-Fi' became 'Wi-Fi', implying that this form of internet access was superior.

702. The Nokia 9000 Communicator was the first internet phone. It launched in Finland in 1996.

703. The Internet of Things, IOT, is the term used for everyday items that connect to the internet.

704. Facebook arrived in 2004, originally only available for college students in the United States, it is now the most popular social media platform in the world.

705. Google went live in '98. Since then, the company has branched into email, its own social network, video sharing, maps and online storage.

706. 'Google' was included in the Oxford English Dictionary in 2006, its definition is "to use the Google search engine to obtain information about the World Wide Web".

707. Online video platform YouTube was founded in 2005, and joined Google in 2006. It was sold for over $1.5 billion. YouTube currently hosts nearly two billion users a month.

708. The first YouTube video was uploaded in April '05, it was titled 'Me at the zoo', and featured Jawed Karim, one of the YouTube founders.

709. The creator of the first website, Tim Berners-Lee has said he has one major regret - the double slash part of website URLS. He has admitted that the '//' serves zero purpose.

710. The word Google comes from 'googol', this is the enormous number shown as a one followed by a hundred zeroes. This reflects the massive amount of data that Google can search through in a matter of seconds.

711. In 2005 Estonia became the first country to allow people to vote over the internet.

712. The right to internet access has been increasingly recognized in state practice in recent years. Estonia classified internet access as a human right in 2001. Finland made broadband a legal right for its citizens in 2009.

713. The internet and the World Wide Web are different things. The internet is made up of a network of computers, and the WWW is the way we access and share information through it.

714. There are over 570 websites created every minute adding up to a total almost 1.8 billion websites since 1991

715. Over 90% of the world's data were created only in the last couple of years.

716. 43% of teachers used online games in the classroom.

717. Over 44 million students or 96% of public schools have computers and access to the internet.

718. 72% of teens feel the need to immediately respond to a text, social media notifications, and other mobile notifications.

719. 48% of parents feel the need to immediately respond to text messages, emails, and social media notifications.

720. Riken Research Lab and Fujitsu developed the Fugaku supercomputer. In June 2020, Fugaku dethroned IBM's Summit supercomputer as the most powerful in the world.

721. Wikipedia is run and maintained by thousands of humans and hundreds of bots. ClueBot NG catches vandalism on Wikipedia pages almost in real time. A variety of other bots contribute standardized data to the online encyclopedia.

722. Symbolics Inc. registered the first .COM domain on March 15, 1985.

723. Nordu.net was technically the first domain name ever but didn't go through the registration process. Less than 15,000 domains had been registered to the web in 1992.

724. In 2010, more than 200 million domains were registered to .COM alone. Dozens of other domain names exist, and millions of websites are registered with each one.

725. Seagate launched the Exos 20+ hard disk drive (HDD) in December 2020. The HDD utilizes HAMR and MACH2 technologies to offer 20 terabytes (TB) of storage.

726. In 2018, the Global Datasphere amounted to 33 Zettabytes of data. Nearly 60% of that data was stored on traditional hard drives.

727. One million recycled laptops save enough energy to power 3,500 homes for a year.

728. Each year, Americans dump cell phones containing worth over $60 million in gold and silver. Americans throw away 14 million mobile devices each year.

729. We blink seven times per minute instead of the usual 20 when using a computer.

730. As of May 2019, more than 500 hours of video were uploaded to YouTube every minute. This equates to approximately 30,000 hours of newly uploaded content per hour.

731. It is estimated that for every 12.5 million spam emails sent out, only one person responds.

732. Samsung was founded as a grocery trading store on March 1, 1938, by Lee Byung-Chull. In the 1960s, Samsung entered the electronics industry.

733. YouTube.com was registered on February 14th, 2005 (Valentine's day) with the purpose of being a video-dating site.

734. Twitter, Wikipedia, and AOL IM all crashed at 3:15pm when Michael Jackson died.

735. Everything you're experiencing right now actually happened 80 milliseconds ago. A study conducted by Dr. David Eagleman at the Baylor College of Medicine found that our consciousness lags 80 milliseconds behind actual events.

THE END

Thank you for reading this book.
I've searched the internet for the most interesting and weirdest facts.
I hope you enjoyed this book and that you learned something new.

ReaverCrest Design books

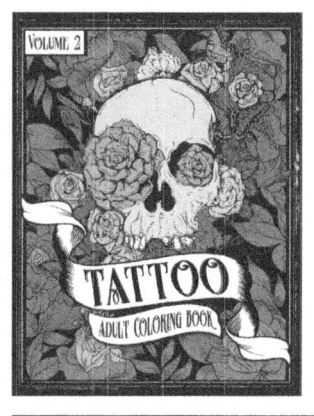

available on Amazon

Made in the USA
Las Vegas, NV
04 December 2022